Beyond Bitcoin:
Exploring Alternative Cryptocurrencies

By

Mary T. Goodnight

TABLE OF CONTENTS

CHAPTER I
Introduction

A. The Rise of Cryptocurrencies

In the last decade, the world witnessed a groundbreaking financial revolution with the emergence of cryptocurrencies. Cryptocurrencies, a form of digital or virtual currency, have reshaped the traditional financial landscape, challenging the very essence of money and the way we conduct transactions. At the forefront of this revolutionary movement stands Bitcoin, the pioneering cryptocurrency that not only introduced the concept of decentralized digital money but also sparked a global frenzy of interest and investment.

Bitcoin, created by an anonymous person or group using the pseudonym Satoshi Nakamoto, made its debut in 2009. As the first cryptocurrency to utilize blockchain technology, Bitcoin offered a novel solution to the longstanding issue of trust in financial transactions. By using cryptographic techniques and a decentralized ledger, it eliminated the need for a central authority, such as a bank, to verify and validate transactions. Instead, the network participants, commonly known as miners, collectively maintained the integrity and security of the blockchain.

The allure of Bitcoin quickly spread across the globe, captivating tech enthusiasts, investors, and even those skeptical of the traditional financial system. Its value soared over the years, reaching unprecedented heights, making early adopters and investors millionaires and, in some cases, billionaires. Bitcoin became synonymous with "digital gold," often seen as a store of value and a hedge against inflation, economic instability, and government interventions.

As Bitcoin's popularity surged, it paved the way for the development of numerous other cryptocurrencies, often referred to as "altcoins" (alternative coins). These alternative cryptocurrencies aimed to address some of the perceived limitations of Bitcoin while exploring new use cases and applications for blockchain technology.

Beyond Bitcoin, a vast and diverse landscape of cryptocurrencies emerged, each with its unique features, use cases, and underlying philosophies. Ethereum, for instance, revolutionized the concept of blockchain by introducing smart contracts, enabling programmable and decentralized applications (DApps). Ripple focused on enhancing cross-border payments and remittances through its fast and efficient payment protocol. Litecoin offered a faster and more scalable alternative to Bitcoin, while Cardano sought to integrate scientific research and academic rigor into its blockchain development. These are just a few examples of the vast array of alternative cryptocurrencies that have sprouted in Bitcoin's wake.

The rise of cryptocurrencies not only disrupted the financial world but also challenged traditional notions of value, ownership, and trust. It prompted debates among economists, regulators, and technology experts, as well as capturing the attention of mainstream media and institutional investors.

In this book, we delve into the world of alternative cryptocurrencies beyond Bitcoin, exploring their technological innovations, potential use cases, investment opportunities, and the challenges they face.

We aim to provide a comprehensive and informative guide that will help readers navigate this rapidly evolving landscape and make well-informed decisions in the exciting and dynamic realm of cryptocurrencies.

As we embark on this journey, it is essential to recognize that the cryptocurrency market is highly volatile and subject to regulatory changes and technological advancements. It is crucial to approach this space with caution, do thorough research, and understand the risks associated with investing and using cryptocurrencies.

Now, let's dive into the intricacies of Bitcoin, examining how it operates and exploring the factors that led to the rise of alternative cryptocurrencies that we see today. By gaining a deeper understanding of these digital assets, we can better grasp the opportunities and potential that lie beyond Bitcoin's boundaries.

B. Bitcoin's Dominance and Limitations

Since its inception, Bitcoin has remained the undisputed leader in the world of cryptocurrencies. As the first and most well-known digital currency, Bitcoin has garnered a significant share of the global cryptocurrency market and continues to dominate discussions surrounding blockchain and decentralized finance. Its journey from a mere concept to a financial powerhouse has been nothing short of remarkable.

Bitcoin's dominance can be attributed to several key factors. First and foremost, its status as the pioneering cryptocurrency gave it a head start in terms of adoption and recognition. Being the first to successfully implement blockchain technology, Bitcoin established the foundation upon which countless other cryptocurrencies would be built.

Additionally, Bitcoin's decentralized nature has been a significant contributing factor to its continued success. Unlike traditional fiat currencies controlled by governments and central banks, Bitcoin operates on a decentralized network of computers distributed worldwide. This decentralization not only makes Bitcoin resistant to censorship and control but also enhances its security, making it virtually tamper-proof.

Furthermore, the limited supply of Bitcoin has played a crucial role in its value proposition. With a capped supply of 21 million coins, Bitcoin is often compared to precious metals like gold, reinforcing its narrative as "digital gold." This scarcity has fueled a sense of digital scarcity, driving demand and contributing to its increasing value over time.

However, despite its undeniable success and contributions to the world of finance and technology, Bitcoin is not without its limitations. One of the most notable drawbacks is scalability. As the popularity of Bitcoin grows, so does the strain on its network. Bitcoin's original block size limit of 1 MB has resulted in slower transaction times and higher fees during peak periods. While several proposals and upgrades have attempted to address this issue, achieving consensus on how best to scale Bitcoin has been a challenge.

Moreover, Bitcoin's consensus mechanism, known as Proof-of-Work (PoW), has also faced criticism for its energy-intensive nature. Mining, the process by which new Bitcoins are created and transactions are verified, requires vast amounts of computational power, leading to concerns about its environmental impact. Discussions about transitioning to more eco-friendly alternatives like Proof-of-Stake (PoS) have emerged, but reaching a consensus on changing a fundamental aspect of Bitcoin's protocol has proven difficult.

Additionally, Bitcoin's use cases have been primarily limited to a store of value and a means of speculative investment. While its role as a store of value is increasingly recognized, its utility as a medium of exchange for everyday transactions is hampered by high transaction fees and slower processing times. This limitation has prompted the development of alternative cryptocurrencies with a focus on enhancing transaction speeds and reducing fees to make everyday use more practical.

In this book, we aim to explore these limitations of Bitcoin and delve into the world of alternative cryptocurrencies that seek to address these challenges. By understanding the strengths and weaknesses of Bitcoin, we can gain valuable insights into the evolving cryptocurrency landscape and the innovative solutions that have emerged to push the boundaries of what digital currencies can achieve.

As we navigate the complexities of Bitcoin's dominance and its limitations, it is crucial to remember that the cryptocurrency market is ever-changing and dynamic. The goal of this book is to provide readers with a comprehensive understanding of both Bitcoin and the diverse world of alternative cryptocurrencies, empowering them to make informed decisions and participate actively in this exciting and transformative financial revolution.

C. The Need for Alternative Cryptocurrencies

While Bitcoin remains the undisputed king of cryptocurrencies, its prominence has also shed light on the need for alternative digital currencies that can address its limitations and cater to a wider range of use cases. The rise of alternative cryptocurrencies, often referred to as "altcoins," is a response to the evolving demands and challenges faced by the cryptocurrency market.

Diversification of Use Cases:

Bitcoin's primary use case as "digital gold" and a store of value has been instrumental in its success, but it also highlights the need for cryptocurrencies that can serve different purposes. The cryptocurrency ecosystem is far from one-size-fits-all, and different industries and users require varied solutions. Alternative cryptocurrencies have emerged to target specific niches and offer innovative features that can transform various sectors, such as finance, supply chain management, healthcare, and more.

Scalability and Transaction Speed:

One of the most significant challenges faced by Bitcoin is its scalability issue. As the number of users and transactions increases, the blockchain network becomes more congested, resulting in slower transaction processing times and higher fees. Alternative cryptocurrencies have sought to tackle this problem by employing different consensus mechanisms and adopting scalable solutions, enabling faster transactions and improving overall network efficiency.

Environmental Concerns:

Bitcoin's energy-intensive Proof-of-Work (PoW) consensus mechanism has raised environmental concerns due to the massive computational power required for mining. As the global focus on sustainability and eco-friendly solutions intensifies, alternative cryptocurrencies employing energy-efficient consensus mechanisms, such as Proof-of-Stake (PoS), have gained popularity. These alternative approaches not only address the ecological impact but also reduce the barriers to participation, making mining more accessible to a broader audience.

Financial Inclusion:

While Bitcoin has provided a secure and decentralized alternative to traditional banking systems, it does not entirely address the issue of financial inclusion for the unbanked and underbanked populations worldwide.

Many alternative cryptocurrencies are designed with a focus on promoting financial inclusivity by providing access to financial services without the need for a traditional bank account. These projects aim to empower individuals in underserved regions and enable cross-border remittances at reduced costs.

Smart Contracts and Decentralized Applications (DApps):

Ethereum's introduction of smart contracts revolutionized the potential use cases for blockchain technology. Smart contracts allow for programmable, self-executing agreements without the need for intermediaries. However, Ethereum's network has also faced scalability challenges. As a result, numerous alternative cryptocurrencies have emerged, offering their platforms for building and deploying decentralized applications. These projects seek to harness the power of smart contracts while addressing the limitations of existing platforms.

Interoperability:

With the increasing number of cryptocurrencies and blockchain networks, the need for seamless interoperability between these platforms becomes evident. Interoperability allows different blockchains to communicate and transfer assets across chains, fostering a more interconnected and efficient decentralized ecosystem. Projects like Polkadot and Cosmos have emerged as notable examples, aiming to create bridges between various blockchains and facilitate data exchange.

In conclusion, the growing need for alternative cryptocurrencies stems from the quest to overcome Bitcoin's limitations and expand the horizons of what blockchain technology can achieve. As the cryptocurrency landscape continues to evolve, these alternative projects play a vital role in driving innovation, offering diverse solutions, and shaping the future of decentralized finance and digital assets.

CHAPTER II
Understanding Bitcoin

A. How Bitcoin Works

Bitcoin, as the first and most well-known cryptocurrency, operates on a decentralized network that utilizes groundbreaking blockchain technology. Understanding how Bitcoin works involves exploring the fundamental principles of blockchain, mining, and transactions.

The Blockchain:

At the heart of Bitcoin lies the blockchain, a distributed and immutable ledger that records all transactions ever made on the network. The blockchain consists of a series of blocks, each containing a list of verified transactions. Every new block is linked to the previous one, forming a chronological chain of transactions. This chain of blocks is secured using cryptographic algorithms, making it nearly impossible to alter past transactions without altering all subsequent blocks, which would require a majority consensus from the network.

Transactions:

Bitcoin transactions are the fundamental building blocks of the blockchain. When a user initiates a Bitcoin transaction, it is broadcasted to the network and included in a pool of unconfirmed transactions. Miners then select transactions from this pool and bundle them into blocks. Each block has a maximum capacity of data it can hold, and transactions compete to be included in the next block based on the fees offered by the sender. Miners prioritize transactions with higher fees, as this incentivizes them to include those transactions first to earn more rewards.

Mining:

Mining is a crucial process that ensures the security and consensus of the Bitcoin network. Miners, acting as decentralized validators, compete to solve complex mathematical puzzles using computational power. The first miner to solve the puzzle gets to create the next block and includes a special transaction known as the "coinbase transaction," which rewards them with newly minted Bitcoins and transaction fees from the included transactions. This process is called Proof-of-Work (PoW) and serves as a mechanism to validate and secure the network while introducing new Bitcoins into circulation.

Consensus:

Consensus is the process by which the Bitcoin network agrees on the validity of transactions and the state of the blockchain. Through mining, miners create blocks and extend the blockchain. To maintain a consistent and single version of the blockchain, all network participants must agree on which chain is valid. This is achieved through the longest-chain rule, where the longest valid chain, with the most accumulated proof-of-work, is considered the valid blockchain.

Wallets:

To participate in the Bitcoin network and manage their funds, users need a digital wallet. Bitcoin wallets come in various forms, such as software wallets, hardware wallets, and paper wallets. These wallets store the user's private keys, which are cryptographic keys required to access and spend their Bitcoins. Transactions on the blockchain are authorized using digital signatures, ensuring the integrity and security of each transaction.

Supply Limit:

One of Bitcoin's defining features is its capped supply. As mentioned earlier, the total number of Bitcoins that can ever be created is fixed at 21 million. This limited supply is built into the protocol to mimic the scarcity of precious metals like gold, making Bitcoin a deflationary asset over time. The gradual release of new Bitcoins through mining, which halves approximately every four years in an event known as the "halving," creates a predictable and diminishing supply schedule.

In conclusion, understanding how Bitcoin works is essential to grasp the underlying principles that have made it a revolutionary digital currency. Its decentralized nature, secured by blockchain technology and validated through mining, has paved the way for a new era of trustless and borderless transactions. As we explore alternative cryptocurrencies beyond Bitcoin, this foundational knowledge of Bitcoin's inner workings will serve as a cornerstone for understanding the diverse and dynamic world of digital assets and blockchain technology.

B. The Advantages and Disadvantages of Bitcoin

Bitcoin, as the pioneer of cryptocurrencies, has garnered significant attention and adoption since its inception. As with any revolutionary technology, Bitcoin comes with its share of advantages and disadvantages, shaping the ongoing debates surrounding its viability and potential impact on the global financial landscape.

Advantages of Bitcoin:

- ❖ Decentralization: One of the most significant advantages of Bitcoin is its decentralized nature. As a peer-to-peer digital currency, it operates on a distributed network of computers worldwide, eliminating the need for a central authority like a bank. This decentralized structure reduces the risk of single points of failure and minimizes the potential for censorship and control.

❖ Security: Bitcoin's blockchain technology is renowned for its robust security. The immutability and cryptographic integrity of the blockchain make it highly resistant to tampering and fraudulent activities. Each transaction on the blockchain is transparent and verifiable, contributing to a high level of trust among users.

❖ Borderless Transactions: With Bitcoin, geographical boundaries become irrelevant. Users can send and receive funds globally without the need for intermediaries or conversion fees associated with traditional cross-border transactions. This feature has significant implications for remittances and international trade.

❖ Limited Supply: Bitcoin's capped supply of 21 million coins gives it an intrinsic scarcity, akin to precious metals like gold. This limited supply and the controlled issuance through mining halvings create a deflationary aspect to the currency, potentially safeguarding against inflationary pressures.

❖ Financial Sovereignty: Bitcoin empowers individuals with financial sovereignty, allowing them to control their funds without reliance on banks or other third parties. Users have full ownership of their private keys, ensuring they have direct control over their assets.

❖ Lower Transaction Fees: In many cases, Bitcoin transactions can be more cost-effective compared to traditional payment methods, especially for international transfers. This is particularly advantageous for cross-border transactions, where conventional methods can incur significant fees and delays.

Disadvantages of Bitcoin:

❖ Scalability: Bitcoin's scalability issue has been a long-standing concern. As the number of users and transactions increases, the network can experience congestion, resulting in slower confirmation times and higher transaction fees. This limitation has led to ongoing debates over potential solutions to improve scalability.

❖ Volatility: Bitcoin's price volatility has been a subject of criticism and caution. While some view this as an opportunity for speculative gains, others see it as a barrier to broader adoption and stability as a medium of exchange.

❖ Environmental Impact: Bitcoin's energy-intensive Proof-of-Work (PoW) consensus mechanism has faced scrutiny due to its significant energy consumption. Critics argue that the electricity consumption associated with mining raises environmental concerns, particularly in an era of increasing awareness about climate change.

❖ Regulatory Uncertainty: The decentralized and borderless nature of Bitcoin has presented challenges for regulators worldwide. Varying regulations and approaches to cryptocurrency create uncertainty for businesses and users, potentially affecting adoption and investment.

❖ Lack of Consumer Protection: Since Bitcoin transactions are irreversible, users need to exercise caution when sending funds. In cases of fraudulent activities or scams, recovering lost funds can be challenging, highlighting the importance of education and security practices.

❖ Adoption and User Experience: While Bitcoin adoption has grown steadily, it is still not widely accepted as a means of payment by all merchants and businesses. Additionally, the user experience for newcomers to the cryptocurrency space can be complex and intimidating, posing a barrier to mainstream adoption.

In conclusion, Bitcoin's advantages and disadvantages contribute to its unique position in the financial ecosystem. Its decentralization, security, and borderless transactions offer compelling benefits, while scalability, volatility, and regulatory challenges present areas for improvement and ongoing discussion. As we explore alternative cryptocurrencies beyond Bitcoin, understanding these pros and cons will serve as a foundation for evaluating the strengths and weaknesses of other digital assets in the dynamic world of blockchain technology.

C. Bitcoin's Impact on the Financial Landscape

Bitcoin's emergence in 2009 marked the beginning of a transformative journey that has had a profound impact on the global financial landscape. As the first decentralized digital currency, Bitcoin has challenged traditional financial systems, redefined the concept of money, and spurred discussions about the future of finance and monetary sovereignty.

Financial Inclusion:

One of the most significant impacts of Bitcoin has been its potential to promote financial inclusion. In regions where traditional banking services are limited or inaccessible, Bitcoin offers an alternative means for individuals to participate in the global economy. With just an internet connection and a digital wallet, anyone can access and transact with Bitcoin, providing newfound financial opportunities to the unbanked and underbanked populations.

Remittances and Cross-Border Payments:

Bitcoin's borderless nature and lower transaction fees have made it an attractive option for remittances and cross-border payments. Migrant workers and expatriates can send money back home more efficiently and affordably using Bitcoin, bypassing intermediaries and avoiding the delays associated with traditional remittance services.

Monetary Sovereignty:

Bitcoin's decentralized nature and limited supply give individuals greater control over their funds. In countries with volatile currencies or unstable financial systems, Bitcoin serves as a store of value and a hedge against inflation and economic instability. This feature grants users greater monetary sovereignty and protection from the devaluation of their wealth.

Disrupting Traditional Finance:

Bitcoin's disruptive potential has raised concerns among traditional financial institutions. As a decentralized and permissionless system, Bitcoin challenges the traditional banking model, where financial intermediaries play a central role. This disruption has prompted debates about the future role of banks and their relevance in a world embracing blockchain technology.

Blockchain Technology:

Bitcoin's underlying technology, blockchain, has garnered significant attention beyond the realm of cryptocurrencies. Blockchain's potential to revolutionize various industries, such as supply chain management, healthcare, and voting systems, has opened up new avenues for innovation and efficiency.

Institutional Adoption:

The increasing adoption of Bitcoin by institutional investors and companies has added legitimacy to the cryptocurrency space. Major corporations, investment firms, and even some governments have expressed interest in Bitcoin as a potential hedge against economic uncertainties and as a diversification strategy for their portfolios.

Regulatory Developments:

Bitcoin's rise has brought about new challenges for regulators worldwide. Governments have grappled with how to address the unique characteristics of cryptocurrencies, ranging from concerns about money laundering and fraud to ensuring consumer protection. Regulatory developments have been both supportive and restrictive, shaping the legal landscape for cryptocurrencies.

Awareness and Education:

Bitcoin's popularity has sparked a global interest in cryptocurrencies and blockchain technology. More individuals are becoming curious about digital assets, leading to increased awareness and education on the subject. Educational initiatives, media coverage, and mainstream discussions have played a crucial role in demystifying cryptocurrencies for the general public.

In conclusion, Bitcoin's impact on the financial landscape has been multifaceted and far-reaching. Its potential to promote financial inclusion, facilitate cross-border transactions, and empower individuals with monetary sovereignty has challenged traditional financial systems. As blockchain technology continues to evolve, the financial world is witnessing a paradigm shift, with Bitcoin at the forefront, leading the way towards a more decentralized and innovative future of finance. As we explore alternative cryptocurrencies beyond Bitcoin, it is essential to understand how this groundbreaking digital asset has shaped the financial world and continues to influence the trajectory of the global economy.

CHAPTER III
Exploring Alternative Cryptocurrencies

A. Ethereum: Smart Contracts and Decentralized Applications

While Bitcoin laid the foundation for cryptocurrencies, Ethereum took the concept of blockchain technology to new heights by introducing the world to smart contracts and decentralized applications (DApps). Created by Vitalik Buterin and launched in 2015, Ethereum quickly gained traction as a versatile platform that expanded the possibilities of what blockchain could achieve.

The Birth of Ethereum:

Ethereum was conceptualized as a platform that would enable developers to build and deploy smart contracts—a self-executing code that automatically enforces the terms of an agreement. This innovation transformed the blockchain from a mere digital currency system to a programmable platform that could support a wide range of decentralized applications and use cases.

Smart Contracts:

At the core of Ethereum's capabilities are smart contracts. These contracts, written in Turing-complete programming languages like Solidity, enable developers to create custom rules and logic for executing agreements without the need for intermediaries. Smart contracts can be used for various purposes, including crowdfunding, escrow services, decentralized governance, and more. Once deployed on the Ethereum network, these contracts are executed automatically when specific conditions are met, ensuring transparency, security, and trust.

Decentralized Applications (DApps):

Ethereum's smart contract functionality paved the way for the development of decentralized applications, or DApps. These applications operate on a peer-to-peer network of computers, removing the need for centralized servers and intermediaries. DApps can cover a vast array of industries, including finance, gaming, supply chain management, and social networking.

The Ethereum Virtual Machine (EVM):

To execute smart contracts and run DApps, Ethereum utilizes the Ethereum Virtual Machine (EVM). The EVM is a runtime environment that enables the execution of code in a sandboxed and secure manner. It ensures that all nodes on the network reach a consensus on the outcome of smart contract execution, preserving the integrity of the blockchain.

Ether (ETH) and Gas:

Ether (ETH) is the native cryptocurrency of the Ethereum network and serves as the fuel for transactions and computational tasks. When users initiate transactions or execute smart contracts on the Ethereum network, they must pay a fee known as "gas." Gas represents the computational power required to process the transaction or contract, and the transaction fee varies based on the complexity and resources consumed.

Ethereum 2.0:

Ethereum has faced scalability and network congestion issues due to its reliance on Proof-of-Work (PoW) for consensus. To address these challenges, Ethereum is transitioning to Ethereum 2.0, a major upgrade that introduces Proof-of-Stake (PoS) as the consensus mechanism. PoS aims to reduce energy consumption and increase network scalability, making Ethereum more efficient and sustainable.

DeFi and Beyond:

Ethereum has become the leading platform for decentralized finance (DeFi) applications. DeFi encompasses a wide range of financial services, including lending, borrowing, decentralized exchanges, and yield farming—all operating on the Ethereum blockchain. The explosive growth of DeFi has attracted considerable attention and investments, shaping the future of financial services.

In conclusion, Ethereum's introduction of smart contracts and decentralized applications has been a game-changer in the cryptocurrency space. Its programmable and versatile blockchain has opened the door to a plethora of innovative use cases and applications, pushing the boundaries of what blockchain technology can achieve.

As Ethereum continues to evolve and transitions to Ethereum 2.0, it remains a significant player in the cryptocurrency ecosystem, inspiring developers and entrepreneurs to explore new frontiers in decentralized applications and financial innovation.

B. Ripple: Revolutionizing Cross-Border Payments

Among the multitude of alternative cryptocurrencies, Ripple stands out as a pioneering digital payment solution with a clear focus on revolutionizing cross-border transactions. Created by Chris Larsen and Jed McCaleb and launched in 2012, Ripple aims to address the inefficiencies and high costs associated with traditional cross-border payment systems, offering a real-time, cost-effective, and secure solution.

The Birth of Ripple:

Ripple, initially known as OpenCoin, was conceived with the vision of creating a decentralized digital currency that could facilitate seamless cross-border transactions. Its core technology, the Ripple Protocol Consensus

Algorithm (RPCA), seeks to improve the speed and cost-effectiveness of global money transfers.

XRP Ledger:

Ripple operates on the XRP Ledger, a decentralized blockchain that serves as the foundation for processing and validating transactions. Unlike many other cryptocurrencies that rely on Proof-of-Work (PoW) or Proof-of-Stake (PoS) for consensus, the XRP Ledger utilizes a unique consensus algorithm known as the Ripple Protocol Consensus Algorithm (RPCA). This consensus mechanism enables fast and efficient transaction validation without the need for energy-intensive mining.

XRP as a Bridge Currency:

At the heart of Ripple's cross-border payment solution lies its native cryptocurrency, XRP. XRP serves as a bridge currency, enabling the seamless exchange of value between different fiat currencies. When a user initiates a cross-border payment, XRP can be used as an intermediary asset, significantly reducing the need for multiple currency conversions and corresponding banking relationships. This feature helps eliminate unnecessary intermediaries and reduces transaction costs and settlement times.

On-Demand Liquidity (ODL):

Ripple's On-Demand Liquidity (ODL) service, formerly known as xRapid, is a key component of its cross-border payment solution. ODL leverages XRP to provide real-time liquidity for international money transfers. Financial institutions can use XRP as a bridge currency, instantly converting funds into XRP and then into the destination currency, facilitating faster and more cost-effective cross-border transactions.

Partnerships and Adoption:

Ripple has formed partnerships with numerous financial institutions, payment service providers, and remittance companies worldwide. These partnerships have led to significant adoption of Ripple's technology for cross-border transactions, with some institutions using

ODL to improve the efficiency of their remittance corridors.

Regulatory Compliance:

Ripple's focus on compliance and adherence to regulatory standards has contributed to its widespread adoption in the financial industry. The company works closely with regulators to ensure compliance with anti-money laundering (AML) and know-your-customer (KYC) requirements, providing added security and trust for its users.

Challenges and Criticisms:

Despite its successes, Ripple has faced challenges, particularly regarding the classification of XRP by regulators. The debate over whether XRP should be deemed a security or not has led to legal issues for the company. Additionally, some critics argue that Ripple's centralized nature, due to its role in the initial distribution of XRP and ongoing sales, contradicts the decentralized ethos of many other cryptocurrencies.

In conclusion, Ripple's innovative approach to cross-border payments has positioned it as a major player in the cryptocurrency space. By leveraging XRP as a bridge currency and offering real-time liquidity through ODL, Ripple has provided a compelling alternative to traditional cross-border payment systems. As the financial industry continues to embrace blockchain technology and seek more efficient solutions for global transactions, Ripple's ongoing efforts to improve the speed, cost, and accessibility of cross-border payments remain instrumental in shaping the future of international finance.

C. Litecoin: Faster and More Scalable than Bitcoin

Litecoin, often referred to as the "silver to Bitcoin's gold," is a prominent alternative cryptocurrency that shares many similarities with Bitcoin but offers distinct advantages, particularly in terms of speed and scalability. Created by Charlie Lee and launched in 2011, Litecoin aims to be a faster and more efficient digital currency for everyday transactions while retaining the fundamental principles of decentralization and security.

The Genesis of Litecoin:

Litecoin was introduced as an open-source project, closely based on the Bitcoin protocol. Charlie Lee, a former Google engineer, sought to create a cryptocurrency that could address some of the perceived limitations of Bitcoin, such as slow transaction confirmation times and high fees.

Scrypt Algorithm:

One of Litecoin's key differentiators is its consensus algorithm. While Bitcoin relies on the energy-intensive Proof-of-Work (PoW) algorithm, Litecoin uses a modified PoW algorithm called Scrypt. Scrypt is memory-intensive rather than computationally intensive, making it less susceptible to specialized mining hardware and more accessible to a broader range of miners.

Faster Block Generation:

Litecoin's block generation time is approximately 2.5 minutes, four times faster than Bitcoin's 10-minute block time. The shorter block time allows Litecoin to process transactions more quickly, enabling faster confirmations and reducing the risk of network congestion during periods of high transaction volume.

Increased Total Supply:

Litecoin has a total supply cap of 84 million coins, four times higher than Bitcoin's 21 million. The increased supply of Litecoin facilitates greater adoption and circulation, as it offers a more abundant pool of coins for transactions. This higher supply also results in smaller unit prices, making it more attractive for micropayments and everyday transactions.

Segregated Witness (SegWit) Implementation:

Litecoin was one of the first cryptocurrencies to implement Segregated Witness (SegWit), a protocol upgrade that optimizes block size and increases transaction capacity. By separating signature data from transaction data, SegWit reduces the size of individual transactions, allowing more transactions to be included in each block. This upgrade significantly improved Litecoin's scalability and lowered transaction fees.

Atomic Swaps and Lightning Network:

Litecoin has actively participated in interoperability efforts and integration with the Lightning Network. Atomic swaps, enabled by both Litecoin and Bitcoin's SegWit implementations, allow for trustless and secure cross-chain exchanges between the two cryptocurrencies. Additionally, the Lightning Network, a layer-two solution that enables fast and low-cost off-chain transactions, further enhances Litecoin's scalability.

Community and Development:

Litecoin has cultivated a dedicated and active community of users and developers. Its strong community support has resulted in consistent development efforts, security updates, and a commitment to improving the cryptocurrency's infrastructure.

While Litecoin shares similarities with Bitcoin, its focus on speed, scalability, and user-friendliness has positioned it as a preferred choice for everyday transactions. As the cryptocurrency space continues to evolve, Litecoin's unique features, active development, and growing adoption make it a noteworthy contender in the competitive landscape of alternative cryptocurrencies. Whether for micropayments, fast transfers, or interoperability with other digital assets, Litecoin's commitment to staying true to the principles of decentralization while advancing its technology demonstrates its potential to be a valuable player in the digital currency revolution.

D. Cardano: Advancing Blockchain Technology through Scientific Philosophy

Cardano, a relatively newer entrant in the world of cryptocurrencies, has quickly gained attention for its unique approach to blockchain technology, emphasizing a scientific and academic-driven philosophy. Launched in 2017 by a team of engineers and academics, including

Charles Hoskinson, one of the co-founders of Ethereum, Cardano aims to be a third-generation blockchain platform, focused on scalability, sustainability, and interoperability.

Scientific Approach:

Cardano's development is grounded in a scientific and research-based methodology. Its team conducts extensive peer-reviewed research, taking inspiration from academic disciplines such as mathematics, cryptography, and game theory. This rigorous scientific approach ensures that every decision and feature implemented on the blockchain is thoroughly studied, tested, and validated before deployment, reducing the likelihood of bugs and vulnerabilities.

Peer-Reviewed Research Papers:

Cardano's commitment to transparency and scholarly validation is evident through its publication of peer-reviewed research papers. These papers explore various aspects of blockchain technology, consensus algorithms, and scalability solutions, providing a level of academic rigor rarely seen in the cryptocurrency space. The academic approach has garnered respect from researchers and institutions, elevating Cardano's reputation in the industry.

Proof-of-Stake (PoS) and Ouroboros:

Cardano employs a PoS consensus mechanism, which significantly reduces energy consumption compared to traditional PoW systems. However, what sets Cardano apart is its Ouroboros protocol—a novel PoS algorithm that was the first to be rigorously analyzed and proven secure through a peer-reviewed process. Ouroboros divides time into epochs and slots, allowing block producers to be selected in a more energy-efficient and secure manner.

Layers of Protocols:

Cardano is designed with multiple layers of protocols to ensure modularity and flexibility. The settlement layer handles the native cryptocurrency ADA and the transfer of value. On top of that, the computation layer enables the execution of smart contracts, similar to Ethereum. By separating these functions, Cardano aims to achieve higher security and efficiency while allowing for future protocol upgrades without disrupting the entire network.

Interoperability and Cross-Chain Communication:

Cardano envisions seamless interoperability between different blockchains. Through its research-focused approach, the project aims to develop protocols for cross-chain communication and collaboration, allowing assets and data to flow freely between different blockchain networks. This interoperability could unlock new use cases and collaborations in the decentralized finance (DeFi) space.

Sustainability and Governance:

Cardano's focus on sustainability extends beyond its scientific development to its governance model. The blockchain implements a treasury system, enabling stakeholders to propose and vote on projects and protocol upgrades. This mechanism allows the community to have a say in the platform's development and ensures that resources are allocated efficiently and sustainably.

Real-World Adoption:

Cardano's ambition to drive real-world adoption is evident in its partnerships and initiatives. The project collaborates with governments, educational institutions, and enterprises to explore blockchain solutions for various sectors, including supply chain management, voting systems, and identity verification.

In conclusion, Cardano's scientific philosophy and academic-driven approach have positioned it as a promising contender in the competitive landscape of alternative cryptocurrencies. By striving to achieve scalability, sustainability, and interoperability, while emphasizing peer-reviewed research, Cardano sets itself apart as a unique and forward-thinking blockchain platform. As it continues to evolve, Cardano's commitment to bridging the gap between academia and blockchain technology may pave the way for innovative and practical solutions with far-reaching impacts across industries and beyond the realm of cryptocurrencies.

E. Polkadot: Interoperability and the Multi-Chain Future

Polkadot, founded by Dr. Gavin Wood, one of the co-founders of Ethereum, represents a groundbreaking advancement in the world of blockchain technology. Launched in 2020, Polkadot aims to address the issue of blockchain interoperability, enabling diverse blockchains to communicate and share data seamlessly. Its ambitious vision centers around creating a network of interoperable chains, fostering a multi-chain future where various specialized blockchains can coexist and collaborate.

The Polkadot Parachain Architecture:

At the heart of Polkadot's interoperability lies its unique parachain architecture. Polkadot serves as a heterogeneous multi-chain framework, where each chain operates as an independent parachain, specialized for specific use cases. These parachains can be customized to suit various applications, such as smart contracts, identity management, decentralized finance (DeFi), and more.

Relay Chain and Consensus:

The Relay Chain acts as the central hub of the Polkadot network, securing the entire ecosystem and facilitating communication between parachains. Polkadot employs a nominated proof-of-stake (NPoS) consensus mechanism, where token holders nominate validators to secure the network and participate in block production. This approach enhances security while maintaining high transaction throughput.

Cross-Chain Communication:

Polkadot's primary innovation is its ability to enable cross-chain communication through the Relay Chain. Parachains can connect to the Relay Chain and interact with other parachains, establishing a cohesive network of interoperable blockchains. This cross-chain communication opens up possibilities for sharing assets, data, and functionalities across chains, fostering a more interconnected and efficient blockchain ecosystem.

Scalability and Shared Security:

Polkadot's design promotes scalability by allowing parallel processing of transactions across multiple parachains. Each parachain can process transactions independently, avoiding bottlenecks and improving overall network throughput. Moreover, by connecting to the Relay Chain, parachains benefit from the shared security and resources of the entire Polkadot network.

Substrate Development Framework:

Polkadot offers a development framework called Substrate, which allows developers to create custom parachains with specific features and functionalities. Substrate simplifies the process of building customized blockchains by providing pre-built modules and tools, reducing development time and costs.

Polkadot's Ecosystem and Projects:

The Polkadot ecosystem has attracted numerous projects and initiatives seeking to leverage its interoperability and scalability features. Projects like Kusama, a canary network of Polkadot, serve as a testing ground for new features and upgrades before being implemented on the main Polkadot network. Additionally, a vibrant community of developers and validators actively contribute to the growth and evolution of the ecosystem.

Future Prospects:

As the blockchain space evolves, Polkadot's multi-chain future offers a compelling vision for the industry. By facilitating seamless communication and collaboration between specialized blockchains, Polkadot paves the way for a more diverse and interconnected blockchain ecosystem, with each chain optimized for specific use cases. This multi-chain approach could lead to greater efficiency, scalability, and innovation across various industries and decentralized applications.

In conclusion, Polkadot's focus on interoperability and its innovative parachain architecture position it as a trailblazer in the realm of alternative cryptocurrencies. By facilitating cross-chain communication and supporting a multi-chain ecosystem, Polkadot aims to unlock new possibilities for blockchain technology, driving the industry toward a more scalable, connected, and versatile future. As the project continues to evolve and attract new participants, its impact on the broader blockchain space remains a key point of interest for developers, enterprises, and the wider cryptocurrency community.

F. Stellar: Enabling Financial Inclusion and Micropayments

Stellar, founded by Jed McCaleb in 2014, is a unique and inclusive blockchain platform that aims to facilitate fast, low-cost, and secure cross-border transactions. Designed with a strong focus on financial inclusion and micropayments, Stellar has garnered attention for its ability to connect individuals, institutions, and payment systems, making it easier for everyone to participate in the global economy.

The Birth of Stellar:

Stellar originated as a fork of the Ripple protocol but underwent significant modifications to better suit its vision for financial inclusion. Jed McCaleb, one of the co-founders of Ripple, sought to create a decentralized platform that could effectively address the needs of the unbanked and underserved populations.

Stellar Consensus Protocol (SCP):

At the core of Stellar's operation lies the Stellar Consensus Protocol (SCP). SCP is a federated Byzantine agreement (FBA) algorithm that enables nodes on the network to reach consensus on the order and validity of transactions. SCP offers high scalability, as it can process thousands of transactions per second, ensuring quick and efficient settlement of payments.

Native Asset: Lumens (XLM):

Stellar's native cryptocurrency is called Lumens (XLM). Lumens play a vital role in the network as an anti-spam measure, preventing malicious users from overwhelming the network with unnecessary transactions. Additionally, Lumens act as a bridge asset, facilitating currency exchange and cross-border transactions between different fiat currencies.

Anchors and Issued Assets:

Stellar's unique feature is its ability to support assets issued by external parties. These assets are typically called "anchors" and represent real-world assets, such as fiat currencies, commodities, or even other cryptocurrencies. Anchors act as a bridge between the Stellar network and the traditional financial system, enabling users to send and receive assets seamlessly.

Stellar Development Foundation (SDF):

Stellar's development and ecosystem are supported by the Stellar Development Foundation (SDF), a non-profit organization dedicated to promoting financial inclusion through the use of blockchain technology. The SDF plays a crucial role in driving adoption, providing grants to developers and projects, and fostering partnerships with various stakeholders in the financial industry.

Focus on Financial Inclusion:

Stellar's primary goal is to enable financial inclusion by connecting individuals and institutions worldwide. By facilitating cross-border transactions and asset issuance, Stellar opens up opportunities for the unbanked and underbanked populations to access essential financial services and participate in the global economy.

Micropayments and Decentralized Exchanges:

Stellar's low transaction fees and fast settlement times make it ideal for micropayments. The platform's focus on financial inclusion also extends to microtransactions, allowing users to transfer even the smallest amounts of value without incurring exorbitant fees.

Partnerships and Real-World Adoption:

Stellar has formed strategic partnerships with numerous organizations, including payment processors, financial institutions, and non-profit organizations. These partnerships have led to real-world adoption of Stellar's technology for cross-border payments, remittances, and other financial use cases.

In conclusion, Stellar's commitment to financial inclusion and its ability to facilitate fast, low-cost cross-border transactions have positioned it as a leading contender in the space of alternative cryptocurrencies. By providing a decentralized platform that connects the unbanked with the global financial system, Stellar has the potential to empower individuals and communities, opening up new opportunities for economic growth and financial empowerment. As Stellar continues to expand its ecosystem and forge meaningful partnerships, its impact on the broader financial landscape remains a compelling aspect to watch for those interested in the future of blockchain technology and digital finance.

H. Other Prominent Altcoins

In addition to the well-known cryptocurrencies like Bitcoin, Ethereum, Ripple, Litecoin, Cardano, Polkadot, Stellar, and Solana, the cryptocurrency space is teeming with a plethora of other prominent altcoins that offer unique features and use cases. While it is impossible to cover every altcoin in detail, this section highlights a few noteworthy projects that have gained attention and popularity in the crypto community.

Binance Coin (BNB):

Binance Coin is the native cryptocurrency of the Binance exchange, one of the largest and most popular cryptocurrency exchanges in the world. BNB was initially launched as an ERC-20 token on the Ethereum blockchain but later migrated to Binance's own blockchain, Binance Smart Chain (BSC). BNB serves various purposes within the Binance ecosystem, including discounted trading fees, participation in token sales, and governance rights.

Chainlink (LINK):

Chainlink is a decentralized oracle network that bridges the gap between smart contracts on blockchain platforms and real-world data. Oracles in the Chainlink network provide secure and reliable off-chain information to smart contracts, enabling them to interact with real-world data and external systems. This feature is crucial for decentralized finance (DeFi) applications, supply chain management, and other use cases that require external data inputs.

Uniswap (UNI):

Uniswap is a decentralized exchange (DEX) built on the Ethereum blockchain that allows users to trade cryptocurrencies without the need for intermediaries. Uniswap uses an automated market maker (AMM) mechanism, enabling liquidity providers to contribute funds to liquidity pools and earn rewards for their contributions. Uniswap's decentralized nature and easy-to-use interface have contributed to its widespread adoption in the DeFi space.

Aave (AAVE):

Aave is a decentralized lending platform that enables users to borrow and lend cryptocurrencies through smart contracts. Aave's unique feature is its implementation of flash loans, which allow users to borrow funds without collateral as long as the loan is repaid within the same transaction. Aave has gained popularity as a leading DeFi lending protocol, offering a wide range of assets and earning opportunities for lenders.

Cardano (ADA):

Cardano is a blockchain platform that aims to provide a more secure and sustainable infrastructure for the development of decentralized applications and smart contracts. Cardano uses a unique proof-of-stake (PoS) consensus mechanism, Ouroboros, which has been thoroughly peer-reviewed to ensure security. Cardano's focus on academic research and peer-reviewed development sets it apart as a highly regarded project in the crypto space.

Dogecoin (DOGE):

Originally created as a joke, Dogecoin has gained a massive following and community support. Despite its humorous origins, Dogecoin has found real-world utility, being used for tipping and charitable donations. Its community-driven nature and fun-loving appeal have contributed to its popularity, making it a significant player in the meme-coin category.

Tezos (XTZ):

Tezos is a self-amending blockchain platform that enables on-chain governance, allowing token holders to propose and vote on protocol upgrades. Tezos uses a PoS consensus mechanism and focuses on formal verification to ensure the security and correctness of smart contracts. Its emphasis on governance and security has garnered attention from enterprises seeking to adopt blockchain technology.

In conclusion, the altcoin space is rich with diverse projects, each offering unique features and use cases. While this section highlights a few prominent altcoins, the cryptocurrency industry is continually evolving, with new projects emerging regularly. Investors and enthusiasts should conduct thorough research and due diligence before engaging with any altcoin, as the market can be highly volatile and subject to changes in regulations and technological developments. As the cryptocurrency ecosystem continues to grow, these altcoins play a vital role in expanding the possibilities of blockchain technology and driving innovation in various industries.

CHAPTER IV
Evaluating the Investment Potential

A. Factors Influencing Cryptocurrency Prices

Investing in cryptocurrencies can be highly rewarding, but it also comes with significant risks due to the volatile nature of the market. Cryptocurrency prices are influenced by a complex interplay of various factors that can lead to rapid price fluctuations. As an investor, it is essential to understand these factors to make informed decisions and manage risks effectively. Here are some key factors influencing cryptocurrency prices:

- ❖ Market Sentiment: Cryptocurrency prices are highly sensitive to market sentiment and investor psychology. Positive news, partnerships, or regulatory developments can drive prices higher, while negative news or security breaches can lead to sharp declines.

- ❖ Supply and Demand: Like any asset, cryptocurrencies are subject to the laws of supply and demand. Limited supply and increasing demand tend to drive prices higher, while a surplus of tokens or declining interest can lead to price corrections.

❖ Technological Development: The technological progress of a cryptocurrency project plays a crucial role in its price performance. Updates, protocol improvements, and the launch of new features can positively impact prices by signaling progress and attracting new investors.

❖ Regulatory Environment: Cryptocurrencies are influenced by the regulatory landscape in different countries. Favorable regulatory developments can boost investor confidence and attract institutional participation, while adverse regulations can hinder growth and lead to price declines.

❖ Market Liquidity: The liquidity of a cryptocurrency affects its price stability. Cryptocurrencies with higher liquidity are less prone to sudden price swings and are more attractive to institutional investors.

❖ Competition: Cryptocurrencies often face competition from other projects within their niche.

Newer and more innovative projects may gain attention, diverting capital and interest from established cryptocurrencies.

❖ Adoption and Use Cases: The real-world adoption of a cryptocurrency and its practical use cases can significantly impact its value. Cryptocurrencies with widespread use and utility are more likely to attract investors seeking tangible benefits.

❖ Media Coverage and Social Media: The media and social media have a powerful influence on cryptocurrency prices. Positive coverage or endorsements from influential figures can drive prices higher, while negative publicity can have the opposite effect.

❖ Macro-economic Factors: Cryptocurrencies are not immune to broader economic trends. Factors such as inflation, interest rates, and geopolitical events can influence investor sentiment and capital allocation.

❖ Market Manipulation: The relatively small size and lack of regulation in the cryptocurrency market make it susceptible to market manipulation. Large holders or groups with significant resources can influence prices through coordinated buying or selling.

❖ Technological Risks: Cryptocurrencies are based on blockchain technology, and vulnerabilities in the code or security breaches can lead to price drops as investor confidence erodes.

In conclusion, investing in cryptocurrencies requires a comprehensive understanding of the factors that influence their prices. Market sentiment, supply and demand dynamics, technological developments, regulations, adoption, and macro-economic factors are all essential considerations for assessing investment potential. As with any investment, thorough research, risk management, and a long-term perspective are crucial to navigating the volatile cryptocurrency market successfully.

B. Risks and Volatility in the Cryptocurrency Market

The cryptocurrency market has gained immense popularity over the years, attracting both retail and institutional investors seeking high returns. However, it is crucial to recognize that investing in cryptocurrencies comes with inherent risks and extreme volatility. Understanding these risks is essential for any potential investor looking to navigate the crypto market. Here are some of the significant risks and volatility factors to consider:

❖ Price Volatility: Cryptocurrencies are notorious for their price volatility. Prices can experience rapid and substantial fluctuations in short periods, often driven by market sentiment, news, and speculative trading.

❖ Lack of Regulation: The cryptocurrency market is relatively young and lacks comprehensive regulation. The absence of clear regulatory frameworks in various jurisdictions can expose investors to potential fraud, market manipulation, and security breaches.

❖ Market Manipulation: The decentralized and largely unregulated nature of the cryptocurrency market makes it susceptible to market manipulation. Pump-and-dump schemes, where the price of a cryptocurrency is artificially inflated and then rapidly sold off, can lead to substantial losses for unsuspecting investors.

❖ Security Risks: Cryptocurrencies are digital assets, and their security depends on the underlying blockchain technology. However, vulnerabilities in smart contracts, exchange hacks, and phishing attacks have resulted in significant losses for investors and institutions.

❖ Technological Risks: Blockchain technology is evolving, and cryptocurrencies are built on complex protocols. Technical bugs, hard forks, and upgrades can lead to unintended consequences, impacting the value of a cryptocurrency.

❖ Regulatory Uncertainty: The regulatory environment for cryptocurrencies varies across different countries and regions. Changes in regulations, or the threat of potential regulations, can cause uncertainty and affect investor sentiment.

❖ Lack of Fundamental Value: Unlike traditional assets, cryptocurrencies often lack intrinsic value or cash flow. Their value is mainly driven by market demand, sentiment, and perceived utility.

❖ Limited Adoption: Although cryptocurrencies are gaining traction, mainstream adoption is still relatively low. Lack of widespread use cases and merchant acceptance can hinder long-term growth.

❖ Market Liquidity: Some cryptocurrencies, particularly smaller or newer ones, may suffer from limited liquidity. Low liquidity can lead to price manipulation, wider bid-ask spreads, and difficulties in executing large trades.

❖ Project Risks: Many cryptocurrency projects are experimental and speculative in nature. Not all projects will succeed, and investors must carefully assess the team's credentials, technology, and overall viability before investing.

❖ High Leverage and Margin Trading: Margin trading and leverage in the crypto market can amplify both gains and losses. Using leverage increases the exposure to price swings, potentially leading to substantial losses.

In conclusion, the cryptocurrency market is highly dynamic and poses significant risks for investors. Extreme price volatility, lack of regulation, security vulnerabilities, and regulatory uncertainty are some of the key risks that require careful consideration. It is essential for investors to conduct thorough research, diversify their portfolios, and only invest what they can afford to lose. Risk management and a long-term perspective are vital for navigating the cryptocurrency market successfully. As the market continues to evolve, it remains crucial for investors to stay informed, exercise due diligence, and be prepared for the inherent risks and uncertainties of the crypto space.

C. The Role of Regulation in Shaping the Crypto Landscape

Regulation plays a pivotal role in shaping the cryptocurrency landscape, impacting market dynamics, investor confidence, and the overall adoption of digital assets. As the popularity of cryptocurrencies has surged, governments and regulatory authorities around the world have grappled with how to approach this emerging asset class. The regulatory environment for cryptocurrencies varies significantly across different countries and regions, and it continues to evolve. Here are some key aspects of the role of regulation in the crypto space:

Investor Protection:

One of the primary goals of cryptocurrency regulation is to safeguard investors from fraudulent schemes, scams, and market manipulation. Regulatory measures, such as know-your-customer (KYC) and anti-money laundering (AML) requirements, are implemented to enhance transparency and reduce the risk of illicit activities in the crypto market.

Market Integrity:

Regulation aims to ensure fair and transparent trading practices, maintaining market integrity and preventing market manipulation. Regulatory frameworks may include measures to combat insider trading, price manipulation, and pump-and-dump schemes that can distort market prices.

Consumer Safety:

Protecting consumers from potential risks associated with investing in cryptocurrencies is a significant concern for regulators. Clear disclosures, risk warnings, and educational initiatives are often put in place to help individuals make informed decisions about cryptocurrency investments.

AML and Counter-Terrorism Financing (CTF):

Regulators often focus on addressing the potential misuse of cryptocurrencies for money laundering and terrorist financing. Robust AML and CTF measures are essential to prevent illicit funds from flowing through the crypto ecosystem.

Taxation:

Taxation of cryptocurrencies is a critical regulatory aspect. Different countries treat cryptocurrencies differently for tax purposes, with some considering them as property, while others categorize them as currency or commodities. Clear taxation guidelines help investors comply with their tax obligations.

Stablecoins and Central Bank Digital Currencies (CBDCs):

Regulators are closely monitoring stablecoins (cryptocurrencies pegged to fiat currencies) and exploring the potential of central bank digital currencies (CBDCs). These initiatives raise considerations related to monetary policy, financial stability, and cross-border transactions.

Licensing and Registration:

Some jurisdictions require crypto-related businesses, such as exchanges and wallet providers, to obtain licenses or register with regulatory authorities. These measures help ensure that businesses operate responsibly and comply with relevant regulations.

Innovation and Technology:

Balancing regulation with technological innovation is a delicate challenge. Regulators seek to foster innovation in the blockchain and cryptocurrency space while also addressing potential risks and ensuring the stability of financial markets.

Global Coordination:

As cryptocurrencies transcend borders, global coordination on regulation is becoming increasingly important. International efforts are underway to develop common standards for cryptocurrencies, fostering cooperation between regulatory bodies worldwide.

Clarity and Certainty:

One of the most significant demands from the crypto community is regulatory clarity and certainty. Ambiguous or conflicting regulations can stifle investment and innovation. Clear and well-defined regulations help create a conducive environment for responsible growth in the crypto industry.

In conclusion, regulation plays a critical role in shaping the crypto landscape. It seeks to strike a balance between fostering innovation, protecting investors, and ensuring market integrity. The evolving regulatory environment will continue to influence the adoption and growth of cryptocurrencies, impacting how investors, businesses, and institutions navigate the rapidly changing crypto space. As the market matures, collaboration between regulators, industry stakeholders, and the crypto community will be key to developing effective and balanced regulatory frameworks that promote the responsible use and integration of cryptocurrencies into the global financial system.

CHAPTER V
Use Cases and Real-World Applications

A. Cryptocurrencies in Financial Services

Cryptocurrencies have rapidly gained traction in the financial services sector, revolutionizing traditional banking, payments, and investment processes. Their unique features, such as decentralization, security, and fast transaction speeds, offer numerous advantages that traditional financial systems struggle to match. Here are some of the key use cases and real-world applications of cryptocurrencies in financial services:

Cross-Border Payments:

Cryptocurrencies have emerged as a compelling solution for cross-border payments, enabling faster and more cost-effective transactions compared to traditional remittance services. By eliminating the need for intermediaries and international banking systems, cryptocurrencies facilitate near-instantaneous transfers between parties located in different countries.

Remittances:

For the millions of people working abroad who send money back home to their families, cryptocurrencies present an efficient alternative to costly remittance services. Cryptocurrencies can significantly reduce fees and transaction times, making it easier for individuals to send and receive funds across borders.

Decentralized Finance (DeFi):

DeFi is a rapidly growing sector within the cryptocurrency ecosystem, offering a wide range of financial services without the need for traditional intermediaries like banks. DeFi platforms enable lending, borrowing, yield farming, decentralized exchanges, and more, all governed by smart contracts and open protocols.

Micropayments:

Cryptocurrencies enable micropayments, allowing for the transfer of tiny amounts of value. This capability has applications in various industries, such as content monetization, pay-per-use services, and Internet of Things (IoT) transactions.

Smart Contracts:

Smart contracts are self-executing agreements with the terms of the contract directly written into code. Cryptocurrencies like Ethereum enable the development and execution of smart contracts, automating complex financial processes and reducing the need for intermediaries.

Tokenization of Assets:

Cryptocurrencies enable the tokenization of real-world assets, such as real estate, art, and commodities. Tokenization fractionalizes ownership, allowing more people to invest in these assets, increasing liquidity, and reducing barriers to entry.

Financial Inclusion:

Cryptocurrencies have the potential to bring financial services to the unbanked and underbanked populations, who lack access to traditional banking systems. With just a smartphone and internet connection, individuals can participate in the global financial system and access essential financial services.

Hedge against Inflation:

In countries experiencing high inflation or economic instability, cryptocurrencies can act as a hedge against loss of purchasing power. People can store their wealth in cryptocurrencies to preserve value during times of economic uncertainty.

Initial Coin Offerings (ICOs) and Security Token Offerings (STOs):

ICOs and STOs allow companies and startups to raise funds by issuing tokens on blockchain networks. This method of fundraising offers a more accessible and decentralized approach to capital raising compared to traditional Initial Public Offerings (IPOs).

Wealth Management and Diversification:

Cryptocurrencies provide investors with additional options for diversifying their portfolios and managing wealth. Including cryptocurrencies in investment strategies can help balance risk and potentially enhance overall returns.

In conclusion, cryptocurrencies have expanded the horizons of financial services, introducing innovative solutions that address long-standing challenges in the traditional financial industry. From cross-border payments to DeFi applications and tokenization of assets, cryptocurrencies offer a wide range of real-world applications. While the adoption of cryptocurrencies in financial services is still in its early stages, their potential to disrupt and improve the financial landscape is increasingly recognized by individuals, businesses, and institutional investors. As the crypto space continues to evolve, further integration of cryptocurrencies into mainstream financial services is likely to reshape the way we transact, invest, and manage our finances in the future.

B. Decentralized Finance (DeFi) and Yield Farming

Decentralized Finance (DeFi) is a revolutionary movement within the cryptocurrency space that aims to transform traditional financial systems by providing open and permissionless financial services. DeFi platforms operate on blockchain networks and smart contracts, removing the need for intermediaries and offering users more control over their assets and financial decisions. One of the most prominent and innovative aspects of DeFi is yield farming. Here's an exploration of DeFi and how yield farming works:

Understanding Decentralized Finance (DeFi):

DeFi refers to a set of financial applications, protocols, and platforms built on blockchain networks like Ethereum. These platforms aim to replicate traditional financial services, such as lending, borrowing, trading, and more, in a decentralized and trustless manner. Users interact with DeFi platforms directly through smart contracts, eliminating the need for intermediaries like banks.

Yield Farming - The Basics:

Yield farming is a concept that emerged within the DeFi ecosystem to optimize returns on cryptocurrencies. In yield farming, users provide liquidity to decentralized liquidity pools by depositing their assets into smart contracts. In return for providing liquidity, users earn rewards, often in the form of additional tokens or fees generated by the DeFi protocol.

Liquidity Provision and Automated Market Makers (AMMs):

Yield farming revolves around liquidity provision in decentralized exchanges (DEXs) that use automated market maker (AMM) protocols. AMMs are smart contracts that enable users to trade cryptocurrencies without relying on order books. Instead, they use liquidity pools created by users who deposit their assets into the pool.

Liquidity Mining and Staking:

To participate in yield farming, users "mine" or "stake" their assets in liquidity pools, effectively becoming liquidity providers. These pools facilitate trading between different cryptocurrencies and earn fees from traders who use the exchange. Liquidity providers earn a share of these fees, as well as additional rewards in the form of tokens issued by the DeFi protocol.

Risk and Reward:

Yield farming can be highly lucrative, offering attractive returns on cryptocurrency holdings. However, it also comes with significant risks. Impermanent loss, smart contract vulnerabilities, and market volatility are some of the risks associated with yield farming. Impermanent loss occurs when the value of the assets in the liquidity pool fluctuates, resulting in potential losses for liquidity providers compared to simply holding the assets.

DeFi Protocols and Governance Tokens:

Many DeFi protocols issue governance tokens that grant users voting rights in the platform's governance decisions. These governance tokens are often distributed to liquidity providers as part of the yield farming rewards. Governance tokens enable users to participate in shaping the future of the DeFi protocol they are invested in.

Expanding DeFi Ecosystem:

The DeFi ecosystem continues to grow rapidly, with new protocols, platforms, and use cases constantly being developed. DeFi has expanded beyond basic lending and borrowing to include complex financial products like synthetic assets, derivatives, and decentralized insurance.

Challenges and Future Outlook:

Despite the immense growth and innovation within the DeFi space, challenges such as scalability, interoperability, and security remain. As DeFi gains more mainstream attention, addressing these challenges will be crucial for the sustainable growth of the DeFi ecosystem.

In conclusion, Decentralized Finance (DeFi) and yield farming have emerged as game-changers in the world of cryptocurrencies and finance. By leveraging blockchain technology and smart contracts, DeFi platforms provide a more open, inclusive, and efficient financial system. Yield farming offers users opportunities to earn rewards and optimize their cryptocurrency holdings by participating in liquidity provision. However, it is essential to approach yield farming with caution, as it involves significant risks and complexities. As the DeFi ecosystem continues to evolve and mature, it holds the potential to revolutionize traditional finance and democratize financial services for individuals around the globe.

C. Non-Fungible Tokens (NFTs): Art, Gaming, and Beyond

Non-Fungible Tokens (NFTs) have taken the world by storm, disrupting various industries with their unique capabilities and potential. NFTs are digital assets that represent ownership or proof of authenticity of a specific item or piece of content on a blockchain. Unlike cryptocurrencies like Bitcoin or Ethereum, each NFT is unique and cannot be exchanged on a one-to-one basis. Instead, they have distinct properties that make them valuable in a wide range of real-world applications. Here are some of the prominent use cases and real-world applications of NFTs:

Digital Art and Collectibles:

One of the most well-known applications of NFTs is in the world of digital art and collectibles. NFTs enable artists to tokenize their digital creations, proving ownership and authenticity. This has led to the rise of digital art marketplaces, where collectors can buy, sell, and trade unique digital artworks as NFTs.

Gaming and Virtual Assets:

NFTs are revolutionizing the gaming industry by enabling true ownership of in-game assets. Gamers can purchase, trade, and sell NFT-based virtual items, such as skins, weapons, and characters. NFTs provide gamers with real value for their virtual assets, unlocking new possibilities for the gaming ecosystem.

Virtual Real Estate:

In virtual worlds and metaverses, NFTs are used to represent virtual real estate and properties. These digital plots of land can be bought and sold as NFTs, allowing users to build, develop, and monetize their virtual properties.

Music and Creative Content:

NFTs offer musicians and content creators new ways to monetize their work and connect directly with their audiences. Musicians can release limited-edition NFTs for albums or exclusive content, while content creators can tokenize their work and provide special benefits to NFT holders.

Intellectual Property Rights:

NFTs provide a robust solution for managing intellectual property rights and royalties. Creators can encode licensing terms and royalty agreements into NFT smart contracts, ensuring that they receive a share of any future sales or usage of their work.

Tokenization of Real-World Assets:

Beyond digital content, NFTs are used to tokenize real-world assets, such as real estate, fine art, luxury goods, and more. Tokenization allows for fractional ownership and increased liquidity, making these assets more accessible to a broader range of investors.

Charity and Social Impact:

NFTs have also found applications in charitable initiatives and social impact projects. NFT auctions and sales have been used to raise funds for various causes, leveraging the uniqueness and collectible nature of NFTs to attract donors.

Virtual Identities and Avatars:

NFTs can represent unique virtual identities and avatars in online communities and virtual worlds. These digital personas can be customized and owned by individuals, providing a sense of identity and ownership in the digital realm.

Supply Chain and Provenance:

NFTs can be used to track the provenance and authenticity of physical goods throughout the supply chain. By tokenizing products or their digital representations, consumers can verify the origin and history of the items they purchase.

Gaming Multiverse:

NFTs have the potential to connect different gaming universes and metaverses, allowing players to transfer their assets and characters seamlessly across various games and platforms.

In conclusion, Non-Fungible Tokens (NFTs) have unleashed a wave of innovation and possibilities across diverse industries. From digital art and gaming to real-world asset tokenization and social impact initiatives, NFTs are transforming the way we create, own, and interact with digital and physical assets. As NFT adoption continues to grow, it opens up new avenues for creators, collectors, investors, and businesses, shaping a more inclusive, decentralized, and creative future. However, as with any new technology, it is crucial to consider the potential challenges, such as copyright infringement, environmental impact, and regulatory scrutiny, to ensure that NFTs are utilized responsibly and sustainably in the long run.

D. Cryptocurrencies in Developing Economies

Cryptocurrencies have shown promise in addressing significant challenges faced by developing economies, providing opportunities for financial inclusion, economic empowerment, and improved financial infrastructure. While these regions often struggle with traditional financial systems, cryptocurrencies offer alternative solutions that can potentially transform the economic landscape. Here are some of the key use cases and real-world applications of cryptocurrencies in developing economies:

Financial Inclusion:

One of the most significant benefits of cryptocurrencies in developing economies is the potential for financial inclusion. In regions with limited access to traditional banking services, cryptocurrencies offer a secure and accessible alternative for individuals to participate in the global financial system. With just a smartphone and an internet connection, people can create crypto wallets and engage in transactions, payments, and remittances.

Cross-Border Transactions and Remittances:

Developing economies often experience high costs and delays in cross-border transactions and remittances. Cryptocurrencies provide a more efficient and cost-effective means for individuals to send and receive funds internationally. By eliminating intermediaries, cryptocurrencies enable near-instantaneous cross-border transfers, significantly reducing fees.

Empowering the Unbanked:

A considerable portion of the population in developing economies remains unbanked, lacking access to formal financial services. Cryptocurrencies can bridge this gap, offering individuals the ability to store and transfer value, access loans, and participate in economic activities without the need for a traditional bank account.

Hedging against Inflation:

Inflation can have severe consequences for economies with unstable or hyperinflated currencies. Cryptocurrencies, with their limited supply and decentralized nature, can act as a store of value and a hedge against currency depreciation. People in regions experiencing high inflation can use cryptocurrencies as a way to protect their wealth.

Access to Investment Opportunities:

Cryptocurrencies provide individuals in developing economies with access to a wide range of investment opportunities beyond traditional financial assets. By investing in cryptocurrencies, people can diversify their investment portfolios and potentially benefit from the growth of the crypto market.

Small Business and E-Commerce:

Cryptocurrencies offer new possibilities for small businesses and e-commerce in developing economies. By accepting cryptocurrencies as payment, businesses can tap into a global customer base and avoid the complexities and fees associated with traditional payment systems.

Humanitarian Aid and Donations:

Cryptocurrencies have been used in humanitarian aid efforts and disaster relief initiatives to provide direct assistance to those in need. Crypto donations can be sent transparently and immediately, helping organizations respond quickly to emergencies.

Transparency and Anti-Corruption Efforts:

Blockchain, the technology underlying cryptocurrencies, offers transparency and immutability. Governments and organizations in developing economies can leverage blockchain to improve transparency, enhance public trust, and fight corruption by ensuring that records and transactions are tamper-proof and accessible to the public.

Decentralized Energy Solutions:

In regions with limited access to reliable energy sources, cryptocurrencies can power decentralized energy solutions. Crypto mining and energy trading platforms based on blockchain technology can provide access to electricity and contribute to energy efficiency efforts.

Improving Financial Infrastructure:

Cryptocurrencies can drive innovation and improvement in the financial infrastructure of developing economies. Blockchain-based solutions can streamline processes like land registry, identity management, supply chain management, and more, leading to greater efficiency and reduced fraud.

In conclusion, cryptocurrencies have the potential to make a profound impact in developing economies, offering solutions to long-standing financial challenges and fostering economic empowerment. Financial inclusion, cross-border transactions, access to investment opportunities, and transparency are just a few of the many ways cryptocurrencies can contribute to the growth and development of these regions. As adoption continues to grow, it will be essential to address regulatory and educational aspects to ensure that cryptocurrencies are used responsibly and to maximize their positive impact on the economies of the developing world.

E. Environmental Impact and Sustainability Concerns

While cryptocurrencies offer a multitude of innovative use cases and real-world applications, their growing popularity has also raised concerns about their environmental impact and sustainability. The energy-intensive nature of cryptocurrency mining and the carbon footprint of blockchain networks have become significant points of discussion among environmentalists, policymakers, and the crypto community. Here are some of the key environmental concerns associated with cryptocurrencies:

Energy Consumption:

The most prominent environmental concern regarding cryptocurrencies is their substantial energy consumption, especially in the case of Proof-of-Work (PoW) consensus mechanisms. PoW requires miners to solve complex mathematical puzzles to validate transactions and add them to the blockchain. This process demands immense computational power, resulting in high electricity consumption.

Carbon Emissions:

The heavy reliance on fossil fuels for electricity generation in some regions exacerbates the environmental impact of cryptocurrency mining. Mining operations powered by coal, natural gas, or other non-renewable sources contribute to carbon emissions, which contribute to climate change and environmental degradation.

E-Waste:

Cryptocurrency mining hardware has a limited lifespan due to rapid technological advancements. As newer and more efficient mining equipment is introduced, older devices become obsolete and add to the growing electronic waste (e-waste) problem.

Mining Centralization:

In PoW-based cryptocurrencies, mining difficulty increases with the network's computational power. As a result, large-scale mining operations and mining pools have gained an advantage, leading to centralization concerns and potential environmental consequences due to the concentration of mining power.

Power Consumption of Nodes:

Beyond mining, running full nodes in cryptocurrency networks also requires significant energy consumption. Full nodes ensure the integrity and security of the blockchain, but they add to the overall energy usage of the network.

Proof-of-Stake (PoS) Solutions:

While PoS consensus mechanisms, such as those used by Ethereum 2.0 and other cryptocurrencies, are touted as more energy-efficient alternatives to PoW, they are not entirely devoid of environmental impact. PoS requires significant computational power and electricity to maintain network security.

Addressing Environmental Concerns:

The cryptocurrency community and blockchain developers are increasingly exploring solutions to mitigate the environmental impact of cryptocurrencies:

Transition to Renewable Energy:

Some cryptocurrency mining operations are shifting to renewable energy sources, such as hydroelectric, solar, or wind power, to reduce their carbon footprint and support sustainability.

Energy-Efficient Algorithms:

Efforts are being made to develop energy-efficient algorithms and consensus mechanisms that require less computational power for validating transactions.

Carbon Offset Initiatives:

Some crypto projects and mining companies are implementing carbon offset initiatives to neutralize their carbon emissions by investing in projects that reduce greenhouse gas emissions.

Green Certifications:

Crypto projects and mining farms can pursue green certifications, demonstrating their commitment to environmentally responsible practices.

Ethereum's Transition to PoS:

Ethereum, one of the most prominent PoW-based cryptocurrencies, is in the process of transitioning to a more energy-efficient PoS consensus mechanism, which is expected to significantly reduce its environmental impact.

In conclusion, while cryptocurrencies have demonstrated transformative potential in various sectors, their environmental impact remains a subject of scrutiny. The energy-intensive nature of cryptocurrency mining and blockchain operations has led to concerns about carbon emissions and e-waste generation. However, the crypto community is actively exploring solutions to address these environmental challenges. Transitioning to renewable energy, adopting energy-efficient algorithms, and embracing PoS consensus mechanisms are some of the steps being taken to promote sustainability. As cryptocurrencies continue to evolve, it is essential for the industry to strike a balance between technological innovation and environmental responsibility, ensuring a sustainable future for both blockchain technology and the planet.

CHAPTER VI
Technical Aspects and Blockchain Innovations

A. Consensus Mechanisms: Proof-of-Work vs. Proof-of-Stake

Consensus mechanisms are fundamental components of blockchain networks, responsible for achieving agreement among participants on the validity of transactions and maintaining the integrity of the distributed ledger. The two most prevalent consensus mechanisms used in blockchain systems are Proof-of-Work (PoW) and Proof-of-Stake (PoS). Each mechanism has distinct characteristics, advantages, and challenges. Let's delve into the differences between PoW and PoS:

Proof-of-Work (PoW):

PoW was introduced by Bitcoin, the first-ever cryptocurrency, and is widely utilized by numerous blockchain networks. In a PoW consensus mechanism, miners compete to solve complex mathematical puzzles using computational power. The first miner to find a valid solution gets to add a new block of transactions to the blockchain and is rewarded with newly minted tokens and transaction fees.

Advantages of PoW:

- Security: PoW is renowned for its robust security, as it requires a significant amount of computational work to modify past transactions.

- Decentralization: PoW encourages a distributed network of miners, preventing any single entity from gaining control over the blockchain.

- Proven Technology: PoW has been battle-tested over the years and demonstrated its resilience in the Bitcoin network.

Challenges of PoW:

- Energy Intensive: PoW mining demands substantial energy consumption, leading to concerns about its environmental impact and carbon footprint.

- Centralization Tendencies: As mining becomes more competitive, larger mining pools may emerge, leading to centralization concerns.

- Scalability: PoW can face challenges in scaling to accommodate a high volume of transactions quickly.

Proof-of-Stake (PoS):

PoS is an alternative consensus mechanism that emerged as a response to the energy-intensive nature of PoW. In a PoS system, validators are chosen to create new blocks based on the number of tokens they "stake" or lock up as collateral. The higher the stake, the higher the chances of being selected to validate transactions and earn transaction fees.

Advantages of PoS:

- Energy Efficiency: PoS requires significantly less energy compared to PoW since there is no competition to solve computational puzzles.

- Reduced Centralization Risk: PoS is designed to incentivize long-term ownership of tokens, reducing the likelihood of centralization by rewarding those who have a vested interest in the network's success.

- Scalability: PoS networks can be more scalable as they don't face the same computational limitations as PoW.

Challenges of PoS:

- Security Concerns: Critics argue that PoS is more susceptible to certain attacks, such as the "Nothing at Stake" problem, where validators can vote on multiple chains simultaneously without risking their tokens.

- Wealth Concentration: PoS may lead to a concentration of wealth and influence among the largest token holders, potentially affecting network governance.

- Fair Distribution: The initial distribution of tokens in a PoS system can be a challenge, as it determines who gets to participate in block validation.

Conclusion:

Both Proof-of-Work and Proof-of-Stake have their merits and shortcomings. PoW is well-established and highly secure but has drawn criticism for its energy consumption. PoS, on the other hand, offers a more energy-efficient and potentially more scalable alternative but faces its own set of challenges, particularly related to security and fair token distribution. As the blockchain space continues to evolve, hybrid consensus mechanisms and novel innovations are being explored to combine the strengths of both PoW and PoS and address their respective weaknesses. Ultimately, the choice of consensus mechanism depends on the specific use case, goals of the blockchain network, and the values of its community.

B. Scalability Solutions: Layer 2 and Beyond

Scalability has been a long-standing challenge for blockchain networks, limiting their ability to process a high volume of transactions quickly and efficiently. As cryptocurrencies gain popularity and adoption increases, the need for scalable solutions becomes even more critical. Several innovative approaches have been developed to address scalability concerns, with Layer 2 solutions and other advancements leading the way. Here's an overview of these scalability solutions:

Layer 2 Solutions:

Layer 2 solutions are protocols or frameworks built on top of existing blockchain networks to improve scalability without compromising on security. These solutions aim to reduce the burden on the main blockchain by processing a group of transactions off-chain and then settling the final result on the main chain.

- Payment Channels: Payment channels, such as the Lightning Network for Bitcoin and Raiden Network for Ethereum, allow users to conduct off-chain transactions instantaneously and at a minimal cost. Only the opening and closing transactions are recorded on the main chain, reducing congestion and increasing scalability.

- State Channels: State channels, like the Connext Network and Celer Network, enable users to interact off-chain while maintaining the ability to settle the final state on-chain. This approach is particularly useful for gaming and other applications that require frequent interactions.

- Sidechains: Sidechains are independent blockchains connected to the main blockchain, allowing assets to move between them through two-way pegs. By shifting some transactions to sidechains, the main blockchain's scalability is improved.

Sharding:

Sharding is a technique used to divide a blockchain network into smaller, more manageable subsets called shards. Each shard processes a portion of the total transactions, allowing the network to process transactions in parallel. Ethereum 2.0, for instance, is transitioning to a sharded architecture to achieve higher throughput and scalability.

Directed Acyclic Graphs (DAGs):

DAGs, used by projects like IOTA and Nano, are an alternative data structure to traditional blockchain. In a

DAG, each transaction validates and confirms previous transactions, forming a directed graph. This approach allows for high scalability and fast transaction processing without the need for miners or blocks.

Optimistic Rollups:

Optimistic rollups are Layer 2 scaling solutions that process transactions off-chain and then submit a cryptographic proof to the main chain, ensuring security and decentralization. Projects like Optimism and Arbitrum are working on implementing this approach to increase Ethereum's scalability.

ZK-Rollups:

Zero-Knowledge (ZK) Rollups combine the benefits of off-chain processing with the security of cryptographic proofs. They aggregate multiple transactions into a single proof, reducing the data that needs to be stored on the main chain while maintaining a high level of security and privacy.

Interoperability:

Interoperability solutions aim to connect different blockchain networks, enabling seamless data and asset transfer between them. Projects like Polkadot and Cosmos utilize interoperability to create a network of blockchains, enhancing scalability by distributing transactions across multiple chains.

Conclusion:

Scalability is a critical aspect of blockchain technology's growth and adoption. Layer 2 solutions, sharding, DAGs, optimistic rollups, ZK-rollups, and interoperability are among the most promising approaches to overcome scalability challenges. These innovations provide avenues for blockchain networks to process a significantly higher number of transactions per second, reducing congestion and transaction fees. As the blockchain space evolves, scalability solutions will continue to be a key focus for developers and researchers, driving the advancement of more efficient and scalable blockchain networks. By combining these solutions and constantly improving the underlying technology, the vision of a decentralized and scalable future for blockchain technology can become a reality.

C. Privacy and Security: Zero-Knowledge Proofs and Beyond

Privacy and security are crucial considerations in the world of blockchain and cryptocurrencies. While blockchain technology offers transparency and immutability, it also exposes transaction details to the public. In response, innovative solutions have been developed to enhance privacy and security, with zero-knowledge proofs (ZKPs) leading the charge. Let's explore how ZKPs and other advancements are shaping privacy and security in the blockchain space:

Zero-Knowledge Proofs (ZKPs):

Zero-knowledge proofs are cryptographic protocols that enable one party (the prover) to demonstrate the truth of a statement to another party (the verifier) without revealing any additional information. ZKPs provide privacy by allowing users to validate transactions without disclosing sensitive data, such as the transaction amount or participants.

- zk-SNARKs (Zero-Knowledge Succinct Non-Interactive Argument of Knowledge): zk-SNARKs are a type of ZKP that allows for highly efficient and compact proofs. They have been successfully implemented in projects like Zcash, enabling private transactions while still maintaining the integrity of the blockchain.

- zk-STARKs (Zero-Knowledge Scalable Transparent Argument of Knowledge): zk-STARKs are another form of ZKP known for their scalability and transparency. They are used in protocols like StarkEx to facilitate private and scalable transactions.

Ring Signatures:

Ring signatures, used by Monero and other privacy-focused cryptocurrencies, enhance transaction privacy by obfuscating the sender's identity. In a ring signature, multiple public keys are combined, making it impossible to determine which one belongs to the actual signer.

Confidential Transactions:

Confidential transactions, employed by projects like Mimblewimble-based cryptocurrencies, hide the transaction amount while still ensuring the transaction is valid. This privacy enhancement conceals the specific amounts being transacted, improving fungibility and reducing the risk of transaction data leakage.

Homomorphic Encryption:

Homomorphic encryption allows computations to be performed on encrypted data without the need for decryption. This approach ensures that sensitive information remains encrypted throughout the computation process, enhancing privacy and security.

Multi-Signature Transactions:

Multi-signature transactions require the approval of multiple parties before funds can be spent. While not inherently privacy-focused, multi-signature schemes add an extra layer of security and control to blockchain transactions.

Bulletproofs:

Bulletproofs are a cryptographic tool that improves the efficiency and privacy of range proofs in confidential transactions. They reduce the size of range proofs, making transactions more compact and efficient while maintaining security.

Secure Multi-Party Computation (MPC):

MPC allows multiple parties to collectively compute a function without revealing their individual inputs. It can be applied to various privacy-sensitive tasks, such as key management and voting, enhancing privacy and security.

Conclusion:

Privacy and security are of utmost importance in the blockchain space, and innovative solutions like zero-knowledge proofs (ZKPs), ring signatures, confidential transactions, homomorphic encryption, and

MPC have revolutionized how transactions are conducted while safeguarding sensitive data. These advancements strike a balance between transparency and privacy, addressing concerns about transactional privacy without compromising the trust and integrity inherent in blockchain technology. As blockchain continues to evolve, further advancements in privacy and security will play a critical role in ensuring that cryptocurrencies and decentralized applications remain secure and user-friendly, enabling the full potential of blockchain technology to be realized.

D. The Interplay of Centralized and Decentralized Elements

In the realm of blockchain technology, the interplay between centralized and decentralized elements has been a topic of extensive discussion. While decentralization lies at the core of blockchain's value proposition, practical considerations often necessitate the incorporation of some centralized components. Striking the right balance between these two paradigms is crucial for building robust and functional blockchain systems. Here's an exploration of the interplay between centralized and decentralized elements in the blockchain space:

Decentralized Consensus:

Decentralized consensus is a hallmark of blockchain networks, allowing participants to reach agreement without relying on a central authority. Consensus mechanisms like Proof-of-Work (PoW) and Proof-of-Stake (PoS) ensure that no single entity controls the validation process, enhancing the security and trustworthiness of the network.

Centralized Governance:

Despite being decentralized in consensus, some blockchain projects incorporate centralized governance mechanisms to manage protocol upgrades and decision-making processes. These governance structures typically involve the participation of stakeholders and community members, but the final authority may still rest with a core development team or foundation.

Decentralized Applications (dApps):

Decentralized applications (dApps) run on blockchain networks, leveraging the decentralized nature of the underlying platform to provide transparency, security, and censorship resistance. dApps interact directly with the blockchain's smart contracts, eliminating the need for intermediaries.

Decentralized Finance (DeFi):

DeFi platforms operate in a decentralized manner, enabling open access to financial services without the need for traditional financial intermediaries. DeFi protocols are governed by smart contracts, making them transparent and resistant to censorship.

Centralized Exchanges (CEX):

Centralized exchanges serve as vital gateways for users to buy, sell, and trade cryptocurrencies. While CEXs offer high liquidity and user-friendly interfaces, they operate under a centralized model, holding custody of users' funds and making them susceptible to hacks and regulatory pressure.

Decentralized Exchanges (DEX):

Decentralized exchanges (DEXs) facilitate peer-to-peer trading of cryptocurrencies without the need for a central intermediary. DEXs use smart contracts to execute trades directly between users, enhancing security and control over funds.

Oracles:

Oracles act as bridges between the blockchain and external data sources, providing smart contracts with real-world information. While oracles serve a crucial role in blockchain applications, they often rely on centralized entities to deliver accurate data.

Privacy Features:

Blockchain projects often integrate privacy features to safeguard user data and transaction details. While these features enhance privacy, the interplay with centralized elements may arise when using off-chain data or third-party privacy solutions.

Regulatory Compliance:

To comply with legal and regulatory requirements, some blockchain projects incorporate centralized identity verification and KYC/AML processes. These measures ensure that users and participants adhere to applicable laws.

Conclusion:

The interplay of centralized and decentralized elements is a dynamic characteristic of the blockchain space. While decentralization provides transparency, security, and censorship resistance, the incorporation of centralized components is often necessary to meet practical needs such as governance, liquidity, and regulatory compliance. Striking the right balance between these elements is essential for building functional and sustainable blockchain ecosystems that leverage the strengths of both paradigms. As the technology continues to evolve, blockchain developers, researchers, and communities will continue to explore innovative solutions that enhance decentralization while addressing real-world requirements. Ultimately, this interplay will shape the future of blockchain technology, determining how it integrates with existing systems and transforms various industries for the better.

CHAPTER VII
The Future of Cryptocurrencies

A. Predictions and Trends for Alternative Cryptocurrencies

The world of cryptocurrencies is constantly evolving, and alternative cryptocurrencies, often referred to as altcoins, have seen significant growth and innovation. As the blockchain space continues to mature, several predictions and trends are shaping the future of these alternative digital assets:

Continued Diversification:

The cryptocurrency market is likely to witness further diversification as new altcoins emerge to address specific use cases and challenges. Projects focused on DeFi, NFTs, privacy, scalability, and interoperability will continue to attract attention and investment.

Decentralized Finance (DeFi) Dominance:

DeFi has become one of the most prominent use cases in the blockchain space, and this trend is expected to continue. DeFi platforms are likely to expand their offerings, providing a wider range of financial services, including lending, borrowing, derivatives, and insurance.

Enhanced Privacy and Security:

Privacy-focused altcoins are gaining traction as users become more concerned about data protection and transaction privacy. Innovations in zero-knowledge proofs (ZKPs), ring signatures, and confidential transactions will continue to enhance privacy features in altcoin projects.

Cross-Chain Interoperability:

Interoperability solutions will play a crucial role in the future of cryptocurrencies. Projects like Polkadot, Cosmos, and bridges between different blockchain networks will enable seamless asset transfer and data exchange across multiple platforms.

Rise of Layer 2 Solutions:

Layer 2 solutions, such as payment channels and state channels, will become more prevalent to address scalability concerns. These off-chain solutions allow for faster and cheaper transactions without compromising security.

Integration of Real-World Assets:

Cryptocurrencies will increasingly represent real-world assets through tokenization. Traditional assets like real estate, fine art, commodities, and stocks will be tokenized on blockchain networks, unlocking new investment opportunities and liquidity.

Environmental Sustainability:

With growing concerns about the environmental impact of cryptocurrencies, projects will focus on implementing more energy-efficient consensus mechanisms and adopting greener practices to address sustainability concerns.

Regulation and Institutional Adoption:

Regulatory clarity will be essential for the widespread adoption of cryptocurrencies. As governments and regulators develop clearer frameworks, institutional investors are likely to enter the market, bringing increased liquidity and legitimacy.

Central Bank Digital Currencies (CBDCs):

The concept of Central Bank Digital Currencies (CBDCs) will gain further traction as central banks around the world explore the idea of digital versions of their fiat currencies. CBDCs will coexist with cryptocurrencies, potentially influencing the global financial landscape.

User-Friendly Wallets and Interfaces:

Improvements in user interfaces and wallet functionalities will make cryptocurrencies more accessible to the general public. User-friendly experiences will encourage broader adoption and usage of altcoins for everyday transactions.

The future of alternative cryptocurrencies is dynamic and promising, driven by ongoing technological advancements, user demands, and regulatory developments. DeFi, privacy solutions, interoperability, and real-world asset tokenization will be significant growth areas. Projects that prioritize sustainability and environmental responsibility will be favored. Moreover, regulatory clarity and institutional adoption will be instrumental in mainstreaming cryptocurrencies. As the industry continues to mature, the potential for blockchain technology and alternative cryptocurrencies to revolutionize finance, governance, supply chains, and various sectors remains vast. However, the road ahead is likely to be filled with challenges, requiring collaboration between industry participants, regulators, and users to ensure a responsible, secure, and innovative future for cryptocurrencies and blockchain technology as a whole.

B. The Role of Governments and Central Banks in Cryptocurrency Adoption

As cryptocurrencies gain traction and become an integral part of the global financial landscape, the role of governments and central banks in shaping their adoption is becoming increasingly significant. The unique nature of cryptocurrencies raises various regulatory and policy considerations, prompting governments and central banks to grapple with the opportunities and challenges presented by this emerging technology. Here's an exploration of the key roles that governments and central banks play in cryptocurrency adoption:

Regulatory Frameworks:

Governments around the world are actively working on formulating regulatory frameworks for cryptocurrencies. These frameworks seek to strike a balance between fostering innovation and protecting investors and consumers. Clear and comprehensive regulations can provide certainty to businesses and investors, encouraging responsible cryptocurrency adoption.

Consumer Protection:

The decentralized nature of cryptocurrencies can expose users to risks such as fraud, hacking, and scams. Governments play a critical role in establishing consumer protection measures, ensuring that cryptocurrency platforms adhere to security standards and safeguarding user funds.

AML and KYC Compliance:

Cryptocurrencies have been associated with money laundering and illicit activities. Governments are working on Anti-Money Laundering (AML) and Know Your Customer (KYC) regulations to combat these risks, requiring cryptocurrency exchanges and service providers to verify customer identities and report suspicious transactions.

Central Bank Digital Currencies (CBDCs):

Several central banks are exploring the concept of Central Bank Digital Currencies (CBDCs) as a form of digital fiat currency. CBDCs have the potential to revolutionize payment systems, monetary policy, and financial inclusion, and their adoption may reshape the cryptocurrency landscape.

Financial Stability and Systemic Risks:

Governments and central banks are assessing the potential systemic risks posed by widespread cryptocurrency adoption. They are closely monitoring the impact of cryptocurrencies on financial stability, as large-scale crypto investments and price fluctuations may have repercussions on traditional financial systems.

Taxation:

Cryptocurrency transactions and investments are subject to taxation in many countries. Governments are developing taxation policies and guidelines to ensure that cryptocurrency users fulfill their tax obligations accurately.

Encouraging Blockchain Innovation:

While some governments approach cryptocurrencies with caution, others are embracing blockchain technology's potential for economic growth and innovation. Governments that support blockchain research and development are likely to foster a more favorable environment for cryptocurrency adoption and industry growth.

International Cooperation:

Cryptocurrencies transcend national borders, requiring international cooperation on regulation and policy. Governments are engaging in dialogues and collaborations to address cross-border challenges and promote harmonized approaches to cryptocurrency adoption.

Financial Inclusion:

Cryptocurrencies have the potential to enhance financial inclusion by providing access to financial services to unbanked and underbanked populations. Governments can support initiatives that leverage cryptocurrencies to bridge the financial inclusion gap and empower underserved communities.

The role of governments and central banks in cryptocurrency adoption is multifaceted, encompassing regulation, consumer protection, financial stability, and the promotion of innovation. Striking the right balance between fostering blockchain technology's potential and mitigating risks is a complex challenge for policymakers. Collaboration between governments, regulators, industry stakeholders, and the cryptocurrency community is crucial for developing responsible and forward-looking approaches to cryptocurrency adoption. As the future of cryptocurrencies unfolds, the role of governments and central banks will continue to evolve, shaping the trajectory of this transformative technology and its integration into the global financial ecosystem.

C. Challenges and Opportunities in Mass Adoption

The mass adoption of cryptocurrencies represents a transformative shift in the global financial landscape, but it also comes with a set of significant challenges and opportunities. As cryptocurrencies continue to gain popularity and recognition, various factors will determine their path to widespread acceptance. Here, we explore the challenges and opportunities that lie ahead in the journey towards mass adoption of cryptocurrencies:

Challenges:

- ❖ Regulatory Uncertainty: One of the most significant challenges is the lack of clear and consistent regulatory frameworks across different jurisdictions. Varying regulations create uncertainty for businesses and investors, hindering widespread adoption.

❖ Security Concerns: The decentralized and pseudonymous nature of cryptocurrencies can make them attractive targets for cyberattacks and fraud. Improving security measures and educating users on best practices will be crucial in mitigating these risks.

❖ Scalability: As more users and transactions enter the cryptocurrency ecosystem, scalability becomes a pressing issue. Current blockchain networks must improve their capacity to handle a higher volume of transactions to support mass adoption.

❖ User-Friendly Interfaces: For mass adoption, cryptocurrencies and blockchain applications must offer intuitive and user-friendly interfaces. Complexity and technical jargon can deter mainstream users from embracing this technology.

- ❖ Volatility: Cryptocurrencies' price volatility poses challenges for adoption as a stable medium of exchange and store of value. Addressing price stability will be essential to instill confidence among potential users.

- ❖ Environmental Impact: The energy-intensive nature of some cryptocurrencies, particularly those using Proof-of-Work consensus, raises concerns about their environmental impact. Sustainable and energy-efficient solutions are needed to address these environmental challenges.

Opportunities:

- ❖ Financial Inclusion: Cryptocurrencies have the potential to provide financial services to the unbanked and underbanked populations worldwide. By leveraging cryptocurrencies, individuals without access to traditional banking can participate in the global economy.

- ❖ Remittances and Cross-Border Payments: Cryptocurrencies can significantly reduce the cost and time of cross-border transactions, making remittances more efficient and accessible for individuals and businesses.

❖ Decentralized Finance (DeFi): DeFi platforms offer innovative financial services without the need for intermediaries, providing opportunities for more inclusive, transparent, and efficient financial systems.

❖ Tokenization of Assets: Tokenization allows real-world assets, such as real estate, art, and commodities, to be represented as digital tokens on the blockchain. This opens up new investment opportunities and liquidity for traditionally illiquid assets.

❖ Central Bank Digital Currencies (CBDCs): The development of CBDCs offers central banks the opportunity to modernize payment systems, enhance monetary policy tools, and foster financial inclusion.

❖ Global Accessibility: Cryptocurrencies enable borderless and instant transactions, making them suitable for individuals and businesses operating in a globalized world.

❖ Blockchain-Based Governance: Cryptocurrencies and blockchain technology can facilitate decentralized governance models, empowering communities to have a say in the projects they support.

Conclusion:

The future of cryptocurrencies lies in their ability to overcome challenges and capitalize on opportunities. Addressing regulatory uncertainties, enhancing security measures, improving scalability, and creating user-friendly interfaces are essential for mass adoption. The potential to promote financial inclusion, revolutionize cross-border transactions, and tokenize real-world assets presents tremendous opportunities for the cryptocurrency space. Collaboration between governments, regulators, industry players, and the wider community is vital to navigate the complexities of the cryptocurrency landscape and create a secure, sustainable, and inclusive future for this transformative technology. As challenges are tackled and opportunities are seized, cryptocurrencies have the potential to revolutionize finance, governance, and various sectors, ushering in a new era of financial empowerment and innovation.

CHAPTER VIII
Navigating the Crypto Space Safely

A. Wallets, Exchanges, and Security Best Practices

As the popularity of cryptocurrencies grows, it is essential for individuals to navigate the crypto space safely. Understanding how to secure your digital assets and interact with wallets and exchanges is crucial to safeguarding your investments and personal information. Here are some security best practices to follow when dealing with wallets, exchanges, and cryptocurrencies:

Choose Secure Wallets:

Selecting the right wallet is the first step in securing your cryptocurrencies. There are several types of wallets available, including hardware wallets, software wallets, and mobile wallets. Hardware wallets, such as Ledger and Trezor, are considered the most secure as they store your private keys offline. Software wallets, like Electrum and Exodus, are also secure but may be vulnerable to malware if used on infected devices. Mobile wallets are convenient for small amounts but may pose security risks if not properly protected.

Use Two-Factor Authentication (2FA):

Enable two-factor authentication (2FA) wherever possible to add an extra layer of security to your accounts. 2FA requires users to provide a second form of verification, typically a unique code sent to their mobile device, in addition to their password. This helps protect your accounts from unauthorized access even if your password is compromised.

Keep Your Software Updated:

Keep your wallet software, operating system, and antivirus programs up-to-date. Regular updates often include security patches that address vulnerabilities, ensuring your devices are better protected against potential threats.

Beware of Phishing Scams:

Be cautious of phishing scams, where attackers impersonate legitimate websites or services to steal your login credentials or personal information. Always double-check URLs and never click on suspicious links or download attachments from unknown sources.

Store Private Keys Securely:

Your private keys are the keys to your cryptocurrency holdings. Never share your private keys with anyone and avoid storing them digitally, especially online. Consider writing them down on paper and storing them in a safe and secure location.

Use Reputable Exchanges:

When using cryptocurrency exchanges to buy, sell, or trade digital assets, opt for reputable and well-established platforms. Conduct thorough research on the exchange's security measures, user reviews, and regulatory compliance.

Withdraw to Secure Wallets:

Avoid leaving large amounts of cryptocurrencies on exchanges. After completing your transactions, withdraw your funds to your secure wallet, where you have full control of your private keys.

Backup Your Wallet:

Regularly backup your wallet to avoid data loss in case of device failure or damage. Keep multiple copies of your backup in safe and separate locations.

Educate Yourself:

Stay informed about the latest security threats and best practices in the crypto space. Educate yourself about different wallet types, cryptographic concepts, and common attack vectors to make informed decisions.

Use Cold Storage for Long-Term Holding:

For long-term holding, consider using cold storage solutions like hardware wallets or paper wallets. These offline storage methods minimize exposure to online threats.

Conclusion:

Navigating the crypto space safely requires a proactive approach to security. Choosing secure wallets, using 2FA, keeping software updated, and avoiding phishing scams are essential steps in safeguarding your digital assets. Additionally, conducting due diligence on exchanges, storing private keys securely, and staying informed about security best practices contribute to a safer and more enjoyable experience in the cryptocurrency world. By following these guidelines and taking the time to educate yourself, you can confidently participate in the crypto space while minimizing risks and protecting your investments.

B. Recognizing Scams and Avoiding Fraudulent Projects

While the cryptocurrency space offers exciting opportunities, it is also a breeding ground for scams and fraudulent projects. As an investor or enthusiast, recognizing scams and avoiding fraudulent schemes is crucial to protect your assets and make informed decisions. Here are some key tips for identifying and steering clear of scams in the crypto space:

Conduct Thorough Research:

Before investing in any cryptocurrency project or participating in an Initial Coin Offering (ICO), conduct thorough research. Look into the team members' backgrounds, the project's whitepaper, and its technology. Be wary of projects with little information available or anonymous teams.

Check Project Legitimacy:

Verify the legitimacy of the project by checking its website, social media presence, and community engagement. Scammers often set up fake websites and social media accounts to deceive potential investors.

Beware of Unrealistic Promises:

Be cautious of projects that make unrealistic promises of high returns or guarantee profits. The cryptocurrency market is highly volatile, and no legitimate project can guarantee specific returns.

Avoid Pump-and-Dump Schemes:

Pump-and-dump schemes involve artificially inflating the price of a cryptocurrency through false or misleading information, then selling it at the peak to unsuspecting investors. Be cautious of sudden price spikes and conduct due diligence before investing.

Look for Red Flags:

Be alert for red flags such as aggressive marketing tactics, unsolicited investment offers, and high-pressure sales tactics. Scammers often use psychological tactics to manipulate individuals into making impulsive decisions.

Stay Away from Pyramid Schemes:

Pyramid schemes involve recruiting others to invest and promising rewards for bringing in new investors. These schemes collapse when there are not enough new participants, leading to losses for the majority of investors.

Avoid Unregulated Exchanges:

Use reputable and regulated cryptocurrency exchanges for buying, selling, and trading digital assets. Unregulated exchanges may not have proper security measures in place, putting your funds at risk.

Verify Credentials:

If someone claims to be a cryptocurrency expert or advisor, verify their credentials and track record. Beware of fake influencers who may promote fraudulent projects for personal gain.

Protect Personal Information:

Never share your private keys, passwords, or sensitive information with anyone. Scammers may attempt to gain access to your funds by posing as customer support representatives or technical experts.

Trust Your Instincts:

If something seems too good to be true or feels suspicious, trust your instincts and walk away. It's better to miss out on an opportunity than to fall victim to a scam.

Navigating the crypto space safely requires vigilance and skepticism. By conducting thorough research, verifying project legitimacy, avoiding unrealistic promises, and staying away from suspicious schemes, you can protect yourself from scams and fraudulent projects. Remember to use reputable exchanges, protect your personal information, and trust your instincts. As the crypto space continues to evolve, staying informed and educated about potential risks will empower you to make wise investment decisions and contribute to the overall safety and integrity of the cryptocurrency ecosystem.

C. Building a Diversified Crypto Portfolio

Building a diversified cryptocurrency portfolio is a prudent strategy to manage risk and maximize potential returns in the volatile crypto market. A well-diversified portfolio can provide exposure to different assets, reduce the impact of individual price fluctuations, and enhance long-term stability. Here are some essential tips for constructing a diversified crypto portfolio:

Research and Due Diligence:

Before creating a portfolio, conduct thorough research on various cryptocurrencies and blockchain projects. Understand their technology, use case, team, market potential, and community support. Consider factors such as adoption, partnerships, and developments to make informed investment decisions.

Asset Allocation:

Determine the allocation of funds among different cryptocurrencies based on your risk tolerance and investment goals. Allocate a higher percentage to well-established cryptocurrencies like Bitcoin and Ethereum, while leaving room for promising altcoins with growth potential.

Core Holdings:

Include core holdings of major cryptocurrencies like Bitcoin and Ethereum. These are often considered the foundation of a diversified portfolio due to their widespread adoption and store-of-value properties.

Mid-Cap and Small-Cap Coins:

Allocate a portion of your portfolio to mid-cap and small-cap coins. These altcoins have higher growth potential but also carry greater risk. Identify projects with solid fundamentals and innovative solutions that address real-world problems.

Stablecoins:

Consider including stablecoins in your portfolio to mitigate risk during periods of high volatility. Stablecoins are pegged to fiat currencies and can act as a hedge against market downturns.

Sector and Use-Case Diversification:

Diversify across various sectors and use cases in the crypto space. For example, allocate to cryptocurrencies in DeFi, NFTs, privacy, scalability, gaming, and other emerging trends.

Dollar-Cost Averaging:

Instead of investing a lump sum, consider dollar-cost averaging. This strategy involves investing a fixed amount at regular intervals, regardless of market conditions. It can help reduce the impact of short-term price fluctuations.

Rebalancing:

Periodically review and rebalance your portfolio to maintain the desired allocation. Market conditions and the performance of individual assets can cause imbalances over time.

Risk Management:

Set clear risk management rules, such as stop-loss levels, to protect your portfolio from significant losses. Risk management is crucial in the crypto space due to its inherent volatility.

Long-Term Perspective:

Cryptocurrency markets can be highly volatile, with price fluctuations in the short term. Adopt a long-term perspective and avoid making impulsive decisions based on short-term price movements.

Conclusion:

Building a diversified cryptocurrency portfolio requires careful consideration and ongoing monitoring. Conduct thorough research, allocate funds based on your risk tolerance and investment goals, and diversify across major cryptocurrencies, mid-cap, and small-cap coins. Consider including stablecoins for risk mitigation and stay up-to-date with market trends and developments. Regularly review and rebalance your portfolio to maintain the desired allocation and adopt a long-term perspective to ride out market fluctuations. A well-diversified crypto portfolio can help you navigate the crypto space safely and position yourself for potential growth and success in the dynamic world of cryptocurrencies.

Conclusion

A. Recapitulating the Journey Beyond Bitcoin

The journey beyond Bitcoin has been an exhilarating exploration of the diverse and dynamic world of cryptocurrencies. In this comprehensive guide, we delved into the foundations of Bitcoin, its rise to prominence, and the limitations that paved the way for alternative cryptocurrencies. We ventured into the realm of Ethereum, Ripple, Litecoin, Cardano, Polkadot, Stellar, Solana, and various other prominent altcoins, discovering their unique attributes and contributions to the crypto space.

Our exploration took us beyond the technology itself, as we recognized the need for alternative cryptocurrencies to address specific use cases and challenges. Decentralized Finance (DeFi) emerged as a dominant force, transforming traditional financial services and opening new avenues for global participation. Non-Fungible Tokens (NFTs) revolutionized art, gaming, and various industries, unlocking digital ownership and creative opportunities like never before.

Throughout this journey, we encountered the challenges and opportunities that come hand in hand with the mass adoption of cryptocurrencies. Regulatory uncertainty, security concerns, and scalability issues were among the challenges we acknowledged. However, we also recognized the immense potential for financial inclusion, cross-border payments, and tokenization of real-world assets.

To navigate the crypto space safely, we armed ourselves with knowledge about wallet security, exchanges, and best practices to avoid scams and fraudulent projects. We understood the importance of building a diversified crypto portfolio, combining core holdings with mid-cap, small-cap coins, and stablecoins for risk management and long-term growth.

As we conclude this journey, it is crucial to emphasize the evolving nature of the cryptocurrency landscape. New projects, technologies, and regulations will continue to shape the future of cryptocurrencies. It is essential to stay informed, adapt to changes, and continue exploring the vast possibilities beyond Bitcoin.

The potential of blockchain technology and cryptocurrencies extends far beyond the realm of finance. From decentralized governance to environmental sustainability, the impact of this technology stretches across industries and borders, driving innovation and reshaping systems.

The journey beyond Bitcoin is an ongoing adventure, and it requires collaboration, responsible decision-making, and a commitment to ethical practices. As we venture into this uncharted territory, let us embrace the potential of cryptocurrencies to empower individuals, foster financial inclusion, and pave the way for a more connected, decentralized, and equitable future.

In closing, let us remember that beyond the buzz and excitement lies a world of transformative possibilities. As we tread the path beyond Bitcoin, let us continue to learn, explore, and contribute to the evolution of this groundbreaking technology, recognizing that each step we take contributes to the collective progress and realization of a decentralized and borderless future.

B. Embracing the Potential of Alternative Cryptocurrencies

As we conclude our journey exploring alternative cryptocurrencies, it becomes evident that the potential of these digital assets extends far beyond the boundaries of conventional finance. The emergence of Bitcoin was a transformative event that paved the way for a diverse ecosystem of blockchain projects, each with its own unique value propositions and innovations. Embracing the potential of these alternative cryptocurrencies offers us a glimpse into a future where decentralized technologies redefine various aspects of our lives.

One of the most significant achievements of alternative cryptocurrencies is their role in expanding financial inclusion. Decentralized Finance (DeFi) platforms enable individuals to access a wide range of financial services, from lending and borrowing to yield farming and liquidity provision, without relying on traditional intermediaries. This empowerment of the unbanked and underbanked populations can foster economic growth and alleviate poverty on a global scale.

Moreover, Non-Fungible Tokens (NFTs) have disrupted the art and gaming industries, revolutionizing how we perceive digital ownership and creativity. NFTs have provided artists and creators with a new revenue stream, while gamers enjoy true ownership of in-game assets. The possibilities for NFTs extend to supply chain management, intellectual property rights, and other areas, indicating their transformative potential across industries.

The evolution of alternative cryptocurrencies also promises to enhance privacy and security in an increasingly digital world. Innovations like zero-knowledge proofs, ring signatures, and privacy-focused altcoins enable users to conduct transactions and interact with blockchain networks without compromising their personal data. These developments hold the key to preserving digital sovereignty and countering the growing threats of cyberattacks and data breaches.

While challenges like regulatory uncertainty and market volatility persist, the potential of alternative cryptocurrencies to revolutionize global finance and disrupt traditional industries remains undeniable. Governments and institutions are taking notice of these transformations, paving the way for the integration of blockchain technology into existing systems.

Embracing the potential of alternative cryptocurrencies requires a forward-thinking mindset, a willingness to adapt, and a commitment to responsible participation. As these technologies continue to evolve, it is crucial to strike a balance between innovation and regulation, ensuring a safe and secure environment for users and investors.

Education and awareness are essential in this journey. Understanding the mechanisms of blockchain, the nuances of different cryptocurrencies, and the risks involved empowers individuals to make informed decisions. With knowledge comes the confidence to navigate the crypto space safely and responsibly.

In conclusion, alternative cryptocurrencies represent the next frontier of technological advancement, promising to disrupt and reshape the world as we know it. From financial services to art, gaming, and beyond, the potential applications of these digital assets are vast and far-reaching. Embracing this potential with caution and foresight will allow us to harness the true transformative power of alternative cryptocurrencies for the betterment of society, economy, and governance. As we move forward, let us embark on this journey with an open mind, a quest for knowledge, and a vision for a decentralized and equitable future.

C. The Ongoing Evolution of the Cryptocurrency Landscape

The cryptocurrency landscape is an ever-evolving ecosystem that continues to captivate the world with its revolutionary potential. Our journey beyond Bitcoin and into the realm of alternative cryptocurrencies has provided us with a glimpse into the dynamic nature of this transformative technology. As we conclude this exploration, it becomes evident that the cryptocurrency space is characterized by continuous innovation, adoption, and adaptation.

From the inception of Bitcoin as the pioneering digital asset, the cryptocurrency market has witnessed a proliferation of diverse projects, each offering unique solutions to real-world challenges. Ethereum introduced smart contracts, unlocking programmable and decentralized applications that have given birth to a thriving DeFi ecosystem. Ripple revolutionized cross-border payments, Litecoin improved transaction speed, and Cardano advanced blockchain technology through scientific philosophy. Polkadot emphasized interoperability, Stellar enabled financial inclusion, and Solana showcased high-speed transactions.

Beyond these prominent altcoins lie a plethora of other projects, each with its aspirations and potential. As the crypto space expands, new use cases, technological advancements, and regulatory developments shape its trajectory. Central Bank Digital Currencies (CBDCs) have emerged as a focal point of interest for governments exploring the possibilities of digitizing their fiat currencies.

In this ongoing evolution, the challenges and opportunities are intertwined. Regulatory frameworks are developing to provide clarity and protect consumers, while ensuring innovation can thrive within appropriate boundaries. Security measures are continuously refined to safeguard against threats and build trust among users and investors. Scalability solutions, privacy enhancements, and environmental sustainability efforts are pursued to address the growing needs of a globalized and conscientious world.

Amidst the transformations, it is essential to remember the core principles that underpin the cryptocurrency movement: decentralization, transparency, and financial empowerment. These principles challenge traditional notions of governance, finance, and ownership, democratizing access to financial services and promoting inclusion.

As we embrace the ongoing evolution of the cryptocurrency landscape, it is crucial to approach this space with discernment and a long-term perspective. Cryptocurrency investments come with inherent risks due to market volatility, but they also offer opportunities for diversification and hedging strategies.

Education and responsible decision-making are essential for individuals seeking to participate in the crypto space. Staying informed about the latest developments, technological advancements, and regulatory changes empowers users to navigate the cryptocurrency landscape safely and make informed choices.

In conclusion, the cryptocurrency landscape is a journey that transcends boundaries, reshapes industries, and empowers individuals. The ongoing evolution of this space will continue to surprise us with its innovations and challenges. As we look towards the future, let us approach this dynamic landscape with curiosity, adaptability, and a commitment to the principles that have driven its transformative potential. By embracing the ongoing evolution of the cryptocurrency landscape responsibly and ethically, we can contribute to a future where blockchain technology and digital assets truly empower individuals and create a more equitable and decentralized global economy.